BARNES & NOBLE BASICS™

saving
Money

by Barbara Loos

3/8/03
$10⁴⁰

Formerly published as
I haven't saved a Dime, Now What?!

**BARNES
& NOBLE
BOOKS**

For information, contact:
Silver Lining Books
122 Fifth Avenue
New York, NY 10011
212-633-4000

Other titles in the **Barnes & Noble Basics**™ series:
Barnes & Noble Basics *Using Your PC*
Barnes & Noble Basics *Wine*
Barnes & Noble Basics *In the Kitchen*
Barnes & Noble Basics *Getting in Shape*
Barnes & Noble Basics *Getting a Job*
Barnes & Noble Basics *Using the Internet*
Barnes & Noble Basics *Retiring*
Barnes & Noble Basics *Using Your Digital Camera*
Barnes & Noble Basics *Getting Married*
Barnes & Noble Basics *Grilling*
Barnes & Noble Basics *Giving a Presentation*
Barnes & Noble Basics *Buying a House*
Barnes & Noble Basics *Volunteering*
Barnes & Noble Basics *Getting a Grant*
Barnes & Noble Basics *Getting into College*
Barnes & Noble Basics *Golf*

introduction

"There is just no way I can save any money,"
my friend, Colleen Stewart, groaned. "I can barely make my
car payments. I don't get it. How do other people save for college, or retirement, or even for that rainy day you hear
so much about?" How, indeed.

When it comes to finances, we know just how scary the
subject can be. That's why we've written **Barnes &
Noble Basics** *Saving Money*. It's designed to walk you
through the puzzling, anxiety-producing world of
money. We've eliminated the jargon and the Wall
Street buzz to show you that learning about finance
needn't be a confusing chore. And we explain how it really is
possible not only to save money, but to invest it wisely, cushion it from taxes, and have some left over for your heirs,
should you so desire. In short, we give you all you need to
know, and no more.

So whether you're fresh out of school or have been working
for years with little to show for it, this book is for you. We
promise painless understanding and tips that you can put to
use right away. So start reading. You soon will see how easy it
really is to save a dime—or two.

Barb Chintz
Editorial Director, the **Barnes & Noble Basics**™ Series

table of contents

Your money

1

YOUR MONEY

❝There is something more powerful than money—knowledge.❞

getting a grip

How to start thinking about money

Congratulations, you're ready to get serious about money. You can do this. It can actually be fun. Think of it as solving a mystery. Once it's solved you'll know how to pay for college, buy a house, a car, or save for a secure retirement. But is the mere thought of saving for retirement setting off a panic attack? Relax, take a deep breath. You are not alone. Personal finance was never taught in high school or college. Imagine how great it would have been if while learning the dates of the Civil War, you also learned how to create a budget or save for retirement.

Even if you know something about money, it can be scary. For starters, it is one of the few things in life that is both a means and an end. In other words, you need money to make money. You can't save a dime unless you have at least a penny to start saving with. Sounds like a set-up, doesn't it? Don't despair. There is something more powerful than money—knowledge. It, too, is both a means and an end. And if used correctly, knowledge will trump money every time. So read on and learn how to harness the power of money to your advantage.

To get started, all you need to know is how much you earn; how much you spend; and the value of what you own. Once you know that, charting your financial goals is easy. Honest.

Still nervous? Don't be. You can hire a professional to help you through this. Skip right to those pages that tell you how to hire a credit counselor (see pages 36–37); how to hire a financial planner (see pages 74–75); how to hire a stockbroker (see pages 86–87); how to hire a tax preparer (see pages 142–143). But if you want to sort out some of these things for yourself, read on.

HOW DO YOU FEEL ABOUT MONEY?

	Yes	No
1. Do you feel that talking about your money concerns with friends is inappropriate?		
2. Do you feel stupid whenever you hear about someone who made a lot of money in the stock market?		
3. Do you think being in debt is okay?		
4. Do you buy on impulse instead of planning your purchases?		
5. Are you worried about your financial security?		
6. Have you avoided reading your employee benefit literature?		
7. Is most of your knowledge about money based on sensational stories you hear or read in the news?		
8. Are you ever surprised at how much money you spend on things, or how high your credit card bill is?		
9. Do you find paying your taxes confusing?		
10. Do you wish you had a filing system for your bills?		

If you answered yes to any of these questions, you are not alone. The subject of money is still taboo to many people. Your fears and concerns can be overcome with a little bit of know-how.

your paycheck

Your paycheck (or pay stub) is a vital piece of your financial life. But it can be a shock to see how much "they" take out of it. Who are "they"? First, your employer takes money out of your **gross** (pre-tax) salary to pay for company "benefits," such as health and dental insurance, and retirement plans, such as 401(k)s. Then your federal, state, and sometimes even local government take money out of your paycheck for taxes and various programs you must contribute to, such as Social Security and Medicare. What you actually get is called your net salary. Pre-tax deductions, such as medical insurance and 401(k) contributions, reduce the amount of salary that you're required to pay taxes on; after-tax deductions come right out of your pocket, no tax benefit there. (See chapter 7 for a whole lot of information on taxes.)

Employee Name	Jane Taxpayer			Social Security No. 010-01-0101	
(A) Earnings	Current Hours	Current Earnings	YTD Hours	YTD Earnings	
Regular Earnings	40.00	811.54	1,520.00	30,330.80	

ACME INDUSTRIES

Total:	40.00	811.54	1,520.00	30,330.80

Taxes	Current Taxes	YTD Taxes	YTD Taxable
(F) Fed Withholding	52.50	3,596.05	29,468.00
(G) Fed FICA Medicare Hospital Ins	11.16	434.35	29,954.90
Fed FICA OASDI	47.69	1,857.20	29,954.00
(H) New Jersey Withholding	65.34	1,279.14	29,468.00
Total:	176.69	7,166.74	

A Regular Earnings: Your weekly or bi-weekly salary or wages. Also called your gross salary.

B Company Medical: What you contribute to have health insurance coverage under your company's medical plan.

C Company Dental: What you contribute to have dental insurance under your company's dental plan.

D Long-term Disability: The amount you pay for coverage under your company's disability insurance program (see page 114).

E 401(k) Savings Plan: The amount of pre-tax money you have deducted from your gross salary to be invested in your company's 401(k) retirement program (see chapter 8).

F Fed Withholding: The amount of federal taxes taken out by your employer and sent to the IRS on your behalf. The amount is based on how many deductions you claimed when you first filled out your W-4 (see chapter 7).

G Fed FICA: What is deducted for federal programs such as Social Security, Medicare, and unemployment insurance.

H State Withholding: Money that is withheld to pay for your state taxes.

Period Beginning 9/08/03	Period Ending 9/14/03	Rate $811.54	
Deductions	Before Tax Deductions	After Tax Deductions	YTD Deductions
Medical—**B**	8.95		377.90
C—Dental	1.00		38.00
Long-term Disability—**D**		.45	18.77
E—401(k)	40.57		486.90
Total:	50.52	.45	921.57
	Current Taxable Benefits	YTD Taxable Benefits	

all about banking

*Check out
your bank
before you
write checks*

Before you can start saving money, you need a place to save it in. If nothing else, you want a bank so you can have direct deposits of your paycheck. This is very common now. And then if you are very brave and very smart, you can set up an automatic transfer of some of your paycheck into your savings account. This is called "paying yourself first"—more about that on page 48.

Be selective in the bank you choose. You want one with inexpensive fees. Many banks charge a small service fee for everyday needs such as cashing checks, using an **ATM** (Automatic Teller Machine), and providing your checks. They charge a lot more for special situations, for example, if you don't keep a minimum balance in your account or you bounce a check—also known as "returned due to insufficient funds." Make sure that the bank you choose is insured by the FDIC—a federal government agency that insures accounts for up to $100,000.

It sounds obvious, but a key way to get a handle on your spending is to go through your checkbook and bank statement every month. Your bank statement contains an itemized statement of your banking activities. It lists all your ATM cash withdrawals, all the checks you wrote, and all the deposits you made. If you take a moment to look through it, you might be surprised by what you learn.

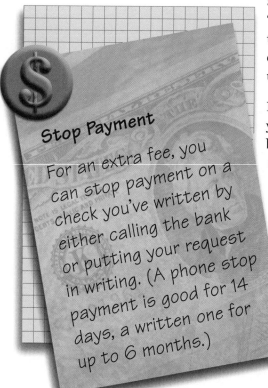

Stop Payment

For an extra fee, you can stop payment on a check you've written by either calling the bank or putting your request in writing. (A phone stop payment is good for 14 days, a written one for up to 6 months.)

TYPES OF BANK ACCOUNTS

Regular checking account: This is your basic checking account. The specifics vary from bank to bank, but often there is no minimum balance requirement, although you may have to pay a monthly service fee. Features can include unlimited check writing, or a certain number of checks can be written per month without additional charge. Generally banks do not pay interest on this type of account, but most do offer overdraft protection in case you do not have funds to cover a check you've written. You'll want to check the interest rate the bank charges for this service before you use it—it can be quite high.

Regular savings account: Another basic service. It lets you deposit checks or cash and pays you a tiny amount of interest on your money. Most people link their savings and checking accounts so they can transfer funds easily from one to the other.

NOW account: This checking account requires that you keep a minimum balance, usually $500. For that you earn a little monthly interest, and there are no monthly fees. **SUPER NOW** accounts require a $2,500 minimum balance and pay higher interest.

Money Market account: This is a special type of checking account that earns greater interest than other types of bank accounts. You also need a larger minimum balance (often $1,000 or more), and usually can write only three checks a month.

banking on-line

Banking any-time you want

The most obvious benefit to on-line banking is that your checkbook will be balanced automatically. Just think—no more waiting for your account statement to arrive in the mail or, for that matter, waiting in line at the bank. You still get a statement in the mail, but you can review your account on-line any time to see recent transactions. To check out on-line banking services across the country and compare rates, take a look at this Internet site: **www.cyberinvest.com**. Click on its Banking Center and choose the Guide to On-line Banks to see how this brave new world of paper-less checks stacks up.

What about security, you ask? Banks take on-line security very seri-ously, especially since even the slightest flaw could severely damage customer confidence. For starters, banks have **fire walls** (computer programs that act as gatekeepers so only known customers get in). When banking on-line you have your own passwords and Personal Identification Numbers (PINs). Passwords make sure you are who you claim to be when you log on; PIN codes verify and confirm each banking transaction that you perform. Thanks to

The CyberInvest Web site is the place to go to locate information about on-line bank-ing services across the country.

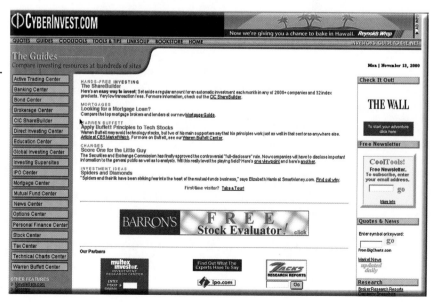

encryption (a process used to convert your data into a series of unrecognizable numbers), none of your personal information (account balances, etc.) can be read over the Internet. Encryption creates a series of numbers that acts as a mathematical lock—a lock to which only your financial institution and browser have the key. And every time you generate a new transaction, a new lock and key combination is created.

ASK THE EXPERTS

How are monthly fees charged for on-line banking?

Monthly fees are typically deducted automatically from your primary checking account (you designate that on the enrollment form) on the date of your statement.

How do I get cash?

If only your computer could magically turn into an ATM! Alas, to get money, you must resort to old-fashioned tactics such as going to a real bank or an ATM machine. (After you open an account, your bank will send you an ATM card and PIN number by the good old mail.) When you withdraw money from an ATM machine, the amount is posted immediately to your on-line account.

How do I deposit money into my account?

Your bank should give you postage-paid, addressed envelopes for mailing your deposits directly to the institution. If they don't, ask for some, or see if you can make deposits with your ATM card. In addition, you can see if your employer will allow you to set up your paycheck for direct deposit (this is recommended by most financial institutions). Then you can simply verify on-line that your check was deposited.

spending habits

Where does the money go?

No matter how big your paycheck, you won't know how much you really have unless you know what you spend it on. This means getting a handle on your expenses. What are expenses? They are anything you spend money on. What most people don't realize is that there are different types of expenses. Mercifully, you can take that into consideration when you begin to draw up a budget. Expenses fall into three categories:

Fixed expenses are essential living expenses that usually do not vary from month to month. These include your rent or mortgage and any sums that must be paid because the law says so, for example, taxes or child support.

Variable expenses are also living expenses, but are not mandated by the government or a legal document such as a lease. They are the things you need to live, such as food, transportation, medical care, and clothes. They vary from month to month. The good news is that by doing a little research, you can usually find less expensive alternatives and save money. More on this in chapter 3.

Nonessential expenses are the little luxuries in life that you think you cannot do without, such as cable TV, movies, café lattes. But the reality is that you probably could. Needless to say, when cutting expenses, these should be the first to go. We'll show you lots of painless ways to do this.

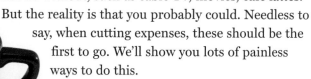

STEP BY STEP: FIGURING OUT YOUR DEBT

How much do you spend on debt each month? This is a quick test to see where you stand debt-wise.

1. Find your last stack of monthly bills. Look for all the fixed expense items. These would be payments you owe every month, such as your rent or mortgage, car payment (but not gas), college loan payment, child support payment. Add those up.

2. Next take a look at your credit card bills. Add the minimum payments you owe. Add the amounts from steps 1 and 2. This is called your *monthly debt obligation.*

3. Figure out your monthly net salary (your take-home pay).

4. Divide your *monthly* fixed expenses by your monthly income. (Take a calculator, punch in the expense number first, hit the divide sign, follow it by the income number.)

5. Ideally, the number you get should be .25 or less. This means that your debt expenses are 25% or less of your income. This is what most financial advisors say is the right percentage. Chances are your number will be higher. (If you are just starting out, housing can take up most of your take-home pay.) Don't be upset. Your percentage is just a way to let you see where you stand.

6. Trimming essential debt is hard to do. But it can be done. We'll show you how in chapter 2. An easier path involves tackling your variable monthly expenses. Turn the page to learn how.

Expenses fall into three types:

✔ fixed expenses

✔ variable expenses

✔ nonessential expenses

tracking expenses

Keeping tabs on what you actually spend

Chances are you are not saving a dime from your monthly income. And whatever big-ticket goals you have, you aren't getting them. You have no idea where your money goes every weekend. Nor do you know why your credit card debt keeps piling up even though you are trying to pay it down. What to do? Keep an account of your expenses. It's the only effective way to know where you are and where you are going financially.

All you need to do is get a little notebook and jot down everything you buy (be it by cash, check, or credit card) every day for a month or two. Everything, even magazines. One of those each week at $3.50 adds up to $182 a year. You may not mind spending that kind of money on magazines, but at least you should know what they are costing you. After a few weeks, you should be able to see these expenses falling into categories that reflect your lifestyle. Once you've noted all the categories, put your daily purchases in the appropriate category. This is called establishing your cash flow. You'll find a sample budget format on page 20. If you are computer-wise, turn to pages 22-23 and see how personal finance software can help you organize and track your spending.

You may find that some of your expenses are taking more than their fair share of your income and represent areas where you can cut back to save. Maybe even 10% of your income! Or you might discover that you are living within your means and the money you want for a house or retirement will have to come from investing (putting money into financial products that earn high interest, see pages 72-73). Or you may want to do a bit of both. The point is that you need to keep track of what you spend, every single dime.

ASK THE EXPERTS

What is disposable income?

It is the money you have left after paying taxes. You can spend this money on essential or nonessential items, or...save it!

I really don't have time to keep track of all my expenses. Is there another way to budget?

If keeping tabs on everything you spend is too painful an exercise, then put a dollar cap on each category of variable expenses. For example, starting with a new month, cap your monthly food budget at $300, your entertainment at $200, etc. You'll still need to keep track of what you spend in these categories, but once you start, you might find it so helpful that you'll be encouraged to keep track of more than you thought possible.

FIRST PERSON   SUCCESS STORY

Budgeting bets can pay off

Keep a budget, keep a budget, that's all my mother ever told me to do. It started in college when I got over my head with credit card charges. And now that I am on my own she keeps harping on it. I told her there was no point to it because I barely make enough money to cover the rent. Finally she bet me $50 that if I kept track of what I spent for two months, I'd find a way to save $50 every month. No way, I said, but what was there to lose? I got a little notebook and started writing down everything I spent. At first it was really a pain, but then it got to be a habit and then after a while it got kind of interesting. It was the little things that surprised me, like how much daily newspapers cost. Or how much dinner and a movie and popcorn could really add up to. After two months, I sat down and put all my entries into categories. And there it was: $50 a month on coffee and bagels. I called my mom and said she'd won. She was so pleased at what I'd done, I didn't have to send her the $50.

Miriam T., Provo, Utah

sample budget

*Organize
your expense
spending*

A budget is an estimate of your income and expenses
over a specified period of time. The key word is estimate. To begin
saving money you need to turn those estimates into real out-of-
your-pocket dollars. That means writing down everything you
spend for a month, preferably three. Start by splitting your notebook into three parts: one for fixed (essential) expenses, the second
for variable expenses, and the third for nonessentials.

1. Categories for fixed expenses are:
rent/mortgage
car payment
car insurance
home insurance
property taxes
child support
school loans
any other loans

2. Categories for variable expenses are:
home maintenance (everything from fixing
the leaky sink to putting up bookshelves)
life insurance
health insurance
car maintenance
gasoline
food
electricity/natural gas
water
phone
childcare

3. Categories for nonessential expenses are on the following page.
These are the ones people often forget to include.

Part 3 nonessentials

	July	August	September
clothes	$72.00	$43.35	$14.95
dry cleaning	23.00	32.50	17.00
shoes	0	92.50	0
café lattes	70.50	75.00	75.00
magazines	3.50	0	9.75
books	19.35	17.25	14.50
movies	15.00	22.50	15.00
wine/liquor	23.00	15.52	17.35
grooming supplies	14.95	13.25	27.52
electronics	0	0	0
music	38.85	0	0
computer games	0	0	0
computer software	0	0	0
dining out	43.50	52.78	103.95
gifts	0	40.00	0
flowers	12.00	50.00	10.00
candy/gum	4.00	5.60	5.00
snacks	12.00	3.75	10.75
cigarettes	0	0	0

money software

Use your computer to help you budget

If you're comfortable using a computer, consider tracking your expenses with personal finance software. Two of the most popular software programs are Microsoft Money and Quicken. (They are available at most computer stores for both PC and Mac and cost under $75.)

What do these programs do for you? Plenty. Most allow you not only to set up a tailor-made tracking system, but also to transfer information about your banking transactions and credit card purchases directly to your budget. For example, the fact that you wrote a check for $45 to your dry cleaner on May 10th will show up in your dry-cleaning expense category. Some software even lets you write and print checks, or, if you prefer, send payments on-line. Another nice feature: it can create a schedule of payments for loans as well as alert you to dates when payments are due. These programs also allow you to track your investments...more on those in chapter 5.

QUICKEN

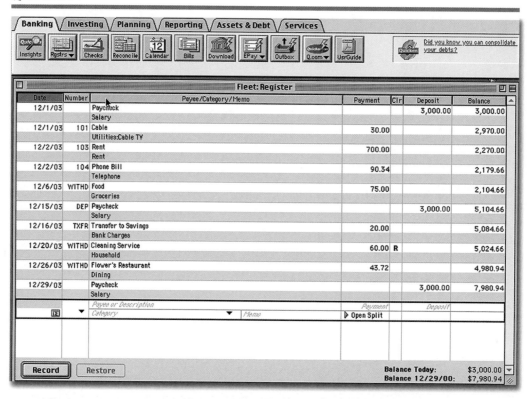

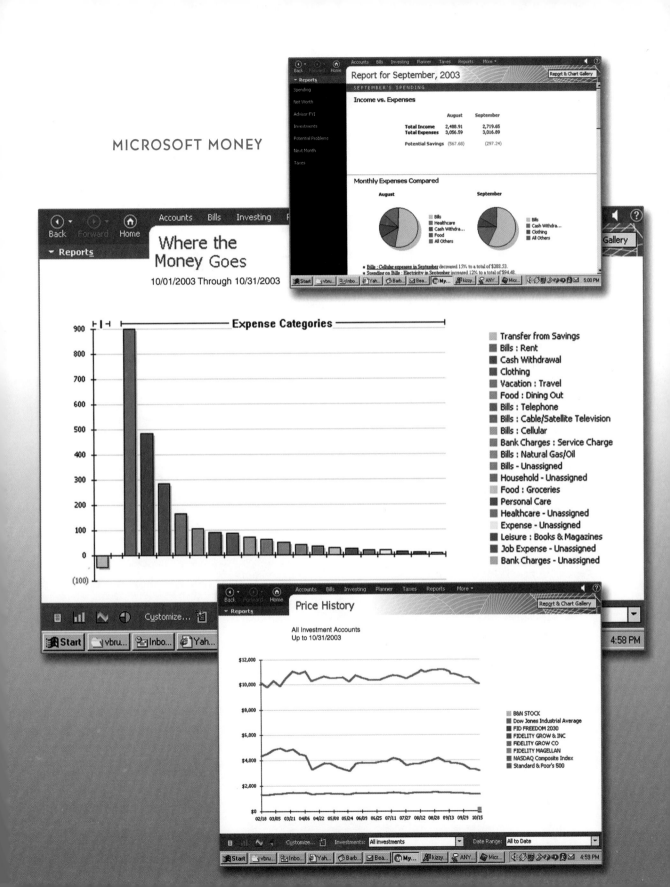

MICROSOFT MONEY

now what do I do?
Answers to common questions

I've just graduated from college and got my first apartment. I can't believe how much it costs. How am I going to save a dime?

You're not alone. This is the typical situation for young people starting out in the real world. The old rule of thumb that your housing should not cost more than 25% of your income has to be tossed out. It usually is more in the 30% to 40% range for young graduates in big cities. That said, the best way to save when starting out is not to over-spend on nonessentials. Credit card debt is so easy to accumulate and so expensive to pay off.

I was really surprised when a check from my boyfriend bounced. But I was even more surprised when my bank charged me $25. Do all banks do that?

Yes. The bank doesn't care whether you wrote the bad check or were the victim of one; they only consider the fact that it bounced. The fee goes to offset the extra process-ing involved in dealing with a bounced check. Some banks charge $15 for a bounced check, others $30. If you have a tendency to be overdrawn a lot and bounce a lot of checks, you might want to consider getting overdraft protection. This is where the bank gives you a credit line to cover the amount you are overdrawn. They usually charge 18% to 22% interest on the amount you owe, so be sure to pay it back immediately.

What about a credit union? My sister raves about hers. Is my money safe there?

Credit unions are a great place to do your banking. Because they are not-for-profit, the fees, loan rates, and charges are lower than those at most banks, and interest on savings is higher. The federal government insures credit-union account deposits up to $100,000, just as it does in a bank account. Many credit unions offer no-fee credit cards that you can pay directly from your checking account. Credit unions are easy to join, but it may take some leg work to track one down if there's no credit union where you work. To find one near you, call the Credit Union National Association at (800) 358-5710.

I'm a freelancer and don't get a regular paycheck. How can I create a budget if I don't know how much I'm going to be getting each month?

A budget is more about getting a handle on your expenses than about your income. Your income may fluctuate from month to month, but chances are your expenses won't. If anything, freelancers need to budget more than others to help pay expenses in those lean months.

I'm not ready for on-line bill paying yet, but I do want to simplify my monthly check writing. Isn't there another way?

Try Electronic Fund Transfers. These programs allow your creditors to withdraw funds automatically from your checking account each month when your bills are due. Not only does this save you the cost of the stamp and the time of writing out the checks, but it also ensures that your bills are paid by the due date—and not before. Contact your bank to set this up; then contact all your monthly creditors, such as the phone company and your mortgage company, and ask them to mail or fax you an electronic transfer form.

ELPFUL RESOURCES

WEB SITES

www.bankrate.com

BOOKS

The Complete Idiot's Guide to Managing Your Money
by Robert K. Heady
and Christy Heady

The Complete Idiot's Guide to Personal Finance
by Eric Tyson

CliffNotes Getting Out of Debt
by Cynthia Clampitt

The Money Tracker: A Quick and Easy Way to Keep Tabs on your Spending
by Judy Lawrence

The Budget Kit: The Common Cents Money Management Workbook
by Judy Lawrence

Getting rid of debt

GETTING RID
OF DEBT

> " Credit cards can
> be invaluable in
> covering a health
> emergency or
> necessary car repair.
> They should not be
> used as mad money
> that stretches your
> buying power. "

credit card overload

It seems so easy to pay the minimum amount due

How much debt is too much? One easy test: if debt is making you feel financially stressed—and some one third of us say they are in this position—it's too much.

What's the problem here? It's called **interest**. When you borrow money, you need to pay for the cost of borrowing it. Why? Because if lenders weren't lending it to you, they could be investing it and earning interest on the investment. You are now their investment, so you get to pay them interest. Banks charge the **prime interest rate** for lending money to their most credit-worthy customers, usually 7% to 10%. When you sign up for a credit card, however, they can charge substantially more, usually from 9% to 21%. They call this their **annual percentage rate**, or APR.

Wait, there's one more tiny problem: it's called **compound interest**. This means that not only will interest be applied to your initial purchase, but also any successive interest you owe. In other words, you will pay interest on interest. Here's an example: say you buy a CD player for $100. You can't pay it all, so you just pay the $10 minimum that first month. Your APR is 18%. When you get your bill for the next month, you will be charged interest on that $90 you still owe. For every day you don't pay the $90 you owe, the interest you now owe compounds. In your second bill, you will be charged 18% on $91.35, not $90. If you don't pay off the CD player for a year, it will wind up costing you $116. Compound interest is a bit like yeast in that it feeds on itself. That's why you don't want to carry credit card debt.

ASK THE EXPERTS

How can I find a cheaper credit card?

On-line financial Web sites make it easy to find competitive interest rates. Two sites that compile a comprehensive range of card deals are www.bankrate.com and www.bestrate.com.

How can I switch my balance to a cheaper card?

After finding the best deal, first tell your current cardholder about it, and ask them to match it. Often they will, because they don't want to lose your business. If not, inform the company you are switching to and they'll explain how to transfer the balance.

What happens if I don't pay my minimum payment?

Not a good idea. As far as the credit card company is concerned, that minimum payment is a loan payment. If you miss the deadline, they report it to the various credit bureaus that keep track of your credit rating, and it is recorded on your credit report (see page 34) as a missed payment. This can hurt your credit rating.

If you make larger purchases just after the monthly closing date for your credit card, you can get a free loan for almost two months. The closing date is the last day that your purchases were recorded for that month's bill. It is usually printed on the bill near the credit and cash advance limits and current balance.

For example: Your card's closing date is August 24, and on August 25 you buy your girlfriend a $150 necklace and earring set for her birthday. When your next bill is issued on about September 3, the charges made after August 24 won't appear on it, so the jewelry charge won't be there. You don't owe anything until the following bill is mailed on October 3. Then you would ideally pay the entire balance by the end of your **grace period** (usually 25 days or so).

Compare that with what happens if you pay a small amount every month for a whole year. At the typical credit card interest rate of 17%, you pay $175 for the same jewelry.

kicking the credit card habit

Avoiding the perils of living on credit

Living beyond your means? You are not alone. It's been the American way of life for years now. A majority of us have maxed out our cards and now just send in the minimum payment each month. The problem is that new credit cards keep arriving in the mail. The debt keeps building. You can't afford to pay it off, but at 18% you can't afford not to!

Help is at hand. You can extricate yourself from your debt mess. The first thing to do is quit denying that you have a credit problem.

STEP BY STEP: CUTTING BACK

1. Shift your debts to the lowest-interest credit card you can find. You can transfer debt from other cards onto a new card. This makes sense if you get a low-interest-rate card.

2. Limit yourself to one card. You don't need more than that. Avoid store cards; they're usually the worst deals of all. The 10% to 20% discount some offer you to sign up is quickly canceled out by the higher interest rates you pay on your purchases.

3. Cancel all other cards. You don't want to leave unused credit cards open. Avoid the temptation; snip the cards and send the issuer a letter informing them you are canceling.

4. Consider a debit card instead of a credit card. A debit card often looks like a credit card, and is just as convenient. But you're not getting credit—the money is immediately subtracted from your checking or savings account. So there are no bills—and no finance fees—to pay at the end of the month. (There are drawbacks to using nothing but a debit card: you don't build a credit rating with it. Also, some cards charge usage fees ranging from 50 cents to $1 per purchase.)

5. Think of credit cards as emergency cash. Cards can be invaluable in covering a health emergency or necessary car repair. They should be used as backup when your ordinary budget plans go awry—not as mad money that stretches your buying power.

6. Draw up a spending budget. (See pages 18–21.) Making your expenses fit pre-set limits is a very effective way to keep debt, especially credit card debt, in check.

WHAT IF I CAN'T CHANGE BY MYSELF

If you have trouble breaking the bad-debt syndrome, consider joining Debtors Anonymous, a national not-for-profit collective where you'll find others working to beat the same problem. There are no dues or fees.

P.O. Box 920888
Needham, MA 02492
Tel: 781-453-2743
www.debtorsanonymous.org
e-mail: new@debtorsanony
mous.org

lightening the load

Getting funds to pay down your debts

Say you're in a bit deep already. Fearsomely deep, even.
There are many things you can do to lighten your load without going deeper into debt. What you need to realize is that the high interest on your credit card debt (15% to 21%) is a crippling expense. You need to find as much money as you can to pay off that debt. The less debt, the lower the interest payments. Here are some ideas:

Ask to trade vacation days for cash. Some companies sometimes let you trade a week or two of vacation for the equivalent salary.

Call in money owed to you. This is the time to ask your brother to repay you for the loan you gave him for that jet ski.

Liquidate your savings. If you have a pile of cash saved, use it to pay off your credit card debt. The interest you are earning on your savings is going to be less than the interest the credit card company is charging you.

Refinance your house. Contact the bank that holds the mortgage on your house and ask about refinancing it and pulling out equity that's built up. Or, get either a second mortgage or an equity line of credit—both give you extra cash and let you pay it back at a lower interest rate than you are paying on your credit cards. (Good news: The interest on mortgages and home equity loans is tax deductible.)

Borrow against your 401(k) (see page 152). The returns you are making on that money are probably much lower than what you're paying for your credit card interest. Simple math dictates that it's smart to pay off a high-interest debt with money that is earning less interest. Whatever you do, don't cash out any retirement savings plans, such as a 401(k) or an IRA, to pay off credit card debt. The tax penalty for doing that is too high.

RESEARCHING LOANS

You can find the best deals by checking financial Web sites. Loanweb, at **www.loanweb.com**, has links to lenders; so does **www.bankrate.com**. The average interest rate for personal loans in late 2002 was about 14.5%.

BORROWING TO BEAT THE DEBT

At first blush, going deeper into debt seems like the last thing you'd want to do. But this makes sense if you can borrow money at a less expensive interest rate than you are paying to the credit card company—and if you stop using the card.

Ask your bank about a personal or consolidation loan. A bank agrees to loan you a lump sum of money, which you use to pay off credit card debts. Then you immediately begin paying back the loan, with interest, in agreed-upon monthly installments. The bank's interest rate and any fees should be lower than your credit card interest. Typically, when a bank makes a loan to you, it assumes that you can dedicate up to 36% of your total gross, not net, income to debt repayment. In other words, if your salary is $50,000, the bank assumes you would use up to $18,000 of your annual net for loan payments.

the credit report

Unraveling your rating

A credit report is a public record of your history of paying your debts. Your credit information is gathered by companies called credit bureaus that sell it to anyone with a legitimate interest in giving you credit: for example, a bank or credit card company. There are three main companies that report on consumers' credit (see box). What's in the report? A list of how much money you've borrowed and from which institution; whether you made payments on time or ever missed a payment; whether you've ever filed for bankruptcy; whether you ever had a credit lien (a creditor's claim against your property, usually your house), and whether you have been sued successfully.

HOW CAN I GET MY CREDIT REPORT?

Write to these three major credit bureaus and ask for a copy. Usually you must pay a small fee.

Experian
(formerly TRW Information Services)
P.O. Box 949
Allen, TX 75013
Tel: 888-397-3742
www.experian.com

Equifax Information Services
P.O. Box 740256
Atlanta, GA 30374
Tel: 800-997-2493
www.equifax.com

Trans Union
P.O. Box 2000
Chester, PA 19022
Tel: 800-888-4213
www.transunion.com

Based on this information they give you a **credit rating** or a formal evaluation of your credit history and your ability to repay future debt. Some bureaus issue a FICO score—a number between 300 (the worst) and 900 (the best) which is assigned to you based on the amount of money you borrowed and the way you repaid it. Most lenders will not lend to you if your score is under 640; a score above 700 is considered good. Others simply note where you missed or were late with a payment, which immediately triggers concern.

A credit bureau sells a copy of your credit report to any institution, such as a bank, credit card or mortgage company, whenever you apply for a loan. (Sometimes they give it to a prospective employer, too). If your credit rating is good, you will get the most favorable rates available. If not, then fixing your credit report should become your number one priority. And if it needs fixing you are not alone. About 70% of consumers in the United States have at least one negative item in their credit reports. If you can explain the problem, say a missed credit card payment due to a hospital stay, you can write down your explanation in 100 words or less and submit copies of it to the three major credit bureaus, and they will attach it to your file. Bad items, such as filing for bankruptcy, stay on your report for 10 years.

CREDIT REPORT

EQUIFAX

Please address all future correspondence to:

Equifax Credit Information Services
P. O. Box 105518
Atlanta, GA 30348
1(800) 882-0648

Personal Identification Information

January 15, 2003

John Jones
100 Main Street
Beecher, NY 00000

Social Security #: 000-00-000
Date of Birth: March 7th, 1955

Credit Account Information

Company Name	Account Number	Whose Acct	Date Opened	Months Reviewed	Date of Last Activity	High Credit	Terms	Balance	Past Due	Status	Date Reported
American Express	00000000000	I	08/86	1	08/98	$0		$0		01	08/98
American Express PAID ACCOUNT/ZERO BALANCE ACCOUNT CLOSED BY CONSUMER	00000000000	I	01/96	4	05/96	$7000		$0		R	06/96
American Residential REAL ESTATE MORTGAGE	00000000000	S	07/88	61	11/94	$41300	380	$0		I1	11/94
Atlantic Mortgage Previous Payment History: 2 Times 90 + days late Previous Status: 07/97 - I5; 06/97 - I5 FORECLOSURE PROCESS STARTED PAID ACCOUNT/ZERO BALANCE	00000000000	I	04/87	2	12/96	$41300	385	$0		I5	01/99
Bank Boston AUTO	00000000000	I	05/93	7	12/93	$7850	207	$0		I1	01/94
UNIS Cash Reserve LINE OF CREDIT AMOUNT IN H/C COLUMN IS CREDIT LIMIT	00000000000		12/94	46	11/98	$2500		$0		R1	11/98
UNIS Home Mortgage Previous Payment History: 1 Time 30 days late Previous Status: 02/97 - I2 ACCOUNT TRANSFERRED OR SOLD REAL ESTATE MORTGAGE	00000000000	I	04/87	26	12/96	$41300	385	$0		I2	03/97
UNIS Manhattan Bank LINE OF CREDIT AMOUNT IN H/C COLUMN IS CREDIT LIMIT	00000000000	J	08/92	48	11/98	$3500	109	$3101		R1	12/98
UNIS Manhattan Bank HOME EQUITY LINE OF CREDIT	00000000000	J	06/96	28	11/98	$73810		$39772		R1	11/98

Creditors will look for any instances of late payments, among other things.

35

getting help

You don't have to find a way out all by yourself

Having trouble with your debt load? Do not go to a private debt doctor who advertises on a telephone pole or on late-night TV. Private companies often charge high fees, and the field is full of charlatans who prey on desperate people. Also avoid private bill-paying services, especially those that claim they can fix up a poor credit record.

And stay calm. There's reasonable, low-cost help to be had. A credit counselor working for a public or not-for-profit agency is the best way to go. For a small fee, the agency typically contacts all of your creditors, negotiates a moratorium on payments to them, and sets up a plan to repay them. But bear in mind that you will be put on a tight leash until it's over; these payments will be made on a fairly aggressive schedule. Your creditors get much of your incoming cash, while you are allowed to keep only an allowance for your essential living expenses.

If this seems frightening, ask the counselor for help in drawing up a budget to see if you can handle the drill. If it looks totally impossible, he can arrange a more lenient payment schedule.

FIRST PERSON   DISASTER STORY

Mother Knows Best

I admit it; I got in way over my head with credit cards. The problem was the more debt I had, the more cards I would get in the mail. If they sent it to me, it must mean it's okay to use. Who knew? By the time I had turned 30, I was in debt for $30,000. It got so bad, I had to move in with my mother to pay it off. It was difficult at first, but she was a good influence on me. She showed me how she was making ends meet on a fixed income by keeping track of what she spent—she even put a little aside each month. Eventually I got my debt down enough so I could get my own place again. I've adopted her good spending and saving habits, and I'm solvent again.

Thomas P., Bronx, New York

ASK THE EXPERTS

Can debt consolidators really fix my bad credit rating?

The answer is no. They may claim they can magically clean up a bad credit report, but that is not true. Only you can clean it up and it's not by using magic. You have to contact each creditor and work out a payment plan. Some may agree to lower your interest rate for this purpose. Once your debts have been paid, you can ask your creditors to report your clean slate to the credit bureaus (see pages 34–35), so your credit history shows your improved status.

How long will it take me to get out of debt?

The answer is usually the same amount of time you have been in debt. In other words, if you have been struggling with too much debt for three years, that's about how long it will take to get clear of it.

Where can I find a credit counselor?

The National Foundation for Consumer Credit is the nation's biggest group of not-for-profit credit counselors. They can direct you to a local office.

Consumer Credit Counseling Services

Tel: 800-547-5005

bankruptcy

*Making a
fresh start*

If all else fails, bankruptcy could be your last resort.
Bankruptcy is a federal proceeding that legally freezes your payment obligations while you either work out a repayment plan to
pay your creditors or petition a court to cancel your debts. The federal government envisions bankruptcy as a "fresh start" for people
who, through misfortune or poor judgment, get totally over their
heads financially and can't get out.

The idea of "going bankrupt" isn't as strange as it used to be.
Personal bankruptcies in the United States have skyrocketed over
the past two decades—from fewer than 200,000 filings in 1978 to a
record high of 1.4 million in 1998. More consumers filed for bankruptcy during the first six months of 1999 than during the entire
decade known as the Great Depression.

Some consumer advocacy groups blame aggressive credit card marketing for this sad state of affairs. Meanwhile, the credit card companies are pressing the government to make it tougher for you to
file for bankruptcy. Why? Because when a consumer goes bankrupt, the card companies and other creditors often don't get paid.

ASK THE EXPERTS

**How do I know if I should consider such a serious step as
bankruptcy?**

One rule of thumb credit counselors use: if your total debt is
more than double your annual income—and if you don't expect
a raise anytime soon—it may be better to file for bankruptcy
than to attempt—perhaps unsuccessfully—to pay your debts.

Will my credit be destroyed for life?

No. But you probably won't be able to borrow for another
six years, and the bankruptcy will stay on your credit report for
10 years. Then it's removed from your file.

STEP BY STEP:
HOW TO FILE FOR PERSONAL BANKRUPTCY

1. Decide which type of bankruptcy to file. Individuals have two choices.

Chapter 7, or "straight" bankruptcy. Your assets (such as a car, house, boat, or expensive equipment) are liquidated; the cash distributed among your creditors; and any remaining debts canceled.

Chapter 13, formerly known as the "wage earners plan." You are allowed to keep your assets and pay back your debts on a two- to five-year schedule that is arranged by a court-appointed trustee. You send the trustee a monthly check, and he pays your creditors.

2. Stop using your credit cards. If the court decides you are running up new debts just to get them covered when you obtain a bankruptcy debt cancellation, they may refuse your bankruptcy petition.

3. If you plan to file on your own, get and read a copy of the U.S. Bankruptcy Code, a useful book that contains the bankruptcy code, rules, and official forms. It's available at libraries and via on-line booksellers. Make sure to get an up-to-date version; the rules change frequently.

4. File your petition on forms provided in the book, or on forms available from a good legal stationery store.

5. If things get confusing, look for a lawyer. Usually the initial consultation is free. (see page 41.)

now what do I do?

Answers to common questions

If my credit card debt is so bad, how come companies keep offering me more credit cards?

Credit card companies have more liberal lending guidelines than banks or other credit institutions. Credit card companies calculate that you can carry debt equal to 36% of your annual gross income, while debt counselors suggest 20%. Credit card companies want you to run up bills because they make their profits from all that interest you're paying. So the more you spend, the more often your mailbox seems to fill up with offers for yet more credit cards from companies eager to take advantage of your penchant for spending.

Which debt should I pay first?

Pay down the most expensive debts first—those with the biggest balances at the highest interest rates, since they're costing you the most. Work your way down to the smallest, lowest-interest debts.

What if there's a mistake on my credit report?

Write a letter to the credit bureau disputing the charge. Send a copy of the letter to the lender who gave out the erroneous information. A summary of your complaint will be put on your credit report. If the lender who gave out the wrong information doesn't respond or dispute it within 30 days, the credit bureau must eliminate it from your report.

What if a creditor is harassing me?

That is against the law. Bill collectors are not allowed to use threats, advertise your debt to the public, or phone you repeatedly about it. If one does, contact the Federal Trade Commission, or FTC. It monitors and investigates complaints about consumer credit practices.

Federal Trade Commission
600 Pennsylvania Ave., NW
Washington, DC 20580
Tel: 877-382-4357
www.consumer.gov or **www.ftc.gov**

Do I need a lawyer to file for bankruptcy?

Though you aren't required to have a lawyer, you are likely to need one. Bankruptcy filings are complex and the ramifications last for years. An experienced bankruptcy attorney can help minimize the damage and maximize all possible benefits. Your local bar association is a good place to turn for a reference. Two organizations that certify bankruptcy lawyers—**The American Bankruptcy Institute** and **The Commercial Law League of America**—also can point you to an attorney in your area.

The American Bankruptcy Institute
44 Canal Center Plaza, Suite 401
Alexandria, VA 22314
Tel: 703-739-0800
www.abiworld.org

The Commercial Law League of America
150 N. Michigan Ave., Suite 600
Chicago, IL 60601
Tel: 312-781-2000
www.clla.org

 # HELPFUL RESOURCES

WEB ADDRESSES

www.loanweb.com

www.bankrate.com

PUBLICATIONS

The Money Diet
by Ginger Applegate

Guide to Understanding Personal Finance
by Kenneth Morris and Alan Siegel

Your Money or Your Life
by Joe Dominguez and Vicki Robin

Savings

3
SAVINGS

"It's important to understand why you're saving, as your goals become the beacon you sail toward."

the magic of interest

Pay to the order of...you

Why save? Two reasons: to achieve your financial goals (whatever they may be) and to weather a financial emergency. The good news is that there is something magical about saving money—the more you save, the more it grows. This is because the **interest** you earn on the **principal**, the money you save or set aside, is also earning interest. This is called **compound interest**. The same principle that hurts your finances if you are in debt helps you if you are saving money, especially if the interest is being compounded daily. It can make all the difference to achieving your financial goals. Consider this: $10,000 invested at 8% for 10 years will have a different **yield** (the money you get from interest), depending on whether the interest is compounded daily, weekly, quarterly, or annually. If it's compounded annually, you will have $21,589 at the end of 10 years. If it's compounded daily, you will have $22,253. That's an additional $664.

What are your goals? Getting a college education? Throwing a big wedding? Buying a house? Having a child? Securing your retirement? All these goals take money, lots of it. If you start saving and harness the power of compound interest, you can get them. Two questions to ask yourself: 1) What are your financial goals? 2) When do you want to achieve them? It all comes down to those two things: time and money.

Experts advise that you start saving as much as you reasonably can, as soon as you can, and put it in a secure investment. There is nothing more depressing than to finally save money, only to lose it on an investment. Once you've accumulated a chunk of change, then you can afford to risk a bit and consider investments that pay higher interest. (Chapter 4 has more about risk and investing.)

WHERE TO INVEST YOUR SAVINGS

If you are just beginning to save, you should put your money in an investment that is as secure as possible. That means there is no **risk** of losing it due to changes in the stock market. For these products, go to a bank or credit union with FDIC insurance and choose from the following:

Money market: the bank pays you higher interest than a traditional savings account. (You also can write two to three checks per month against it.)

Certificate of deposit or CD: the bank holds your money and pays you a set interest rate for a pre-determined period of time, usually one, two, three, or six months, or one, two, three, or five years. There are penalties for early withdrawals.

Money Market Mutual Fund: a mutual fund company invests your money in extremely short-term bonds (see page 98). This is another option that is secure, but not guaranteed. Its characteristics are similar to a bank money market account, but it pays slightly more because it is not insured. (See pages 68-69 regarding risk and reward.)

emergency savings

The right cache for your cash

Why an emergency fund, you ask? Because it can mean the difference between a comfortable life and an uncomfortable one should a financial emergency strike. Having an emergency money fund can cushion you against unexpected blows to your wallet, such as losing your job, getting a divorce, or totaling your car.

How much do you need to stash away? You need enough to cover your living expenses for at least three months. If you are self-employed and your income is erratic, you should reserve enough to cover six months of expenses.

Not possible! you cry. Okay. You don't have to sock it away all at once. Put it on your list of saving goals and be sure to make progress on this one.

Whatever you save should be kept **liquid**, meaning you should be able to get it easily. Put it in a money market account (see page 13). Interest on money markets can be twice as high as interest on savings accounts, and you can take out money at a moment's notice. So before you save for anything else, start with an emergency fund. Once you have that comfortable cushion, forget about it. It is not to be touched, not even to help with a down payment on a house.

Rain Check

There I was, happy as an account manager at my job and then, wham, my company merges and the next thing I know I am out of job. I was totally shocked! The worst part was that I only got three months' severance pay. Even so, I thought I could get a job pretty quickly and maybe stash the severance away in my savings. No such luck. I had forgotten how long it takes to get a job. Just updating my resumé took a week. Then there's all the networking and ads to reply to, not to mention waiting for interviews. My outplacement counselor said to add a month to your job search for every $10,000 of salary. By her account it would take four months for me to get employed. The only good news was that I had saved some money away for a rainy day— about two months' worth of expenses. When I finally did land a job, I still had some money left over. I kept it where it was and immediately started to add to my rainy day fund. You never know when you're going to need it.

Isaac K., Sioux City, Iowa

ASK THE EXPERTS

I have my emergency money in a one-year CD. What happens if I need it before then?

You can withdraw the money, but you'll have to pay an early withdrawal penalty for taking it out before the CD reaches its maturity date. Penalties vary from bank to bank; some charge three months' interest, others six months'. You're usually better off keeping emergency funds in a money market account since those accounts do not have penalties for withdrawals.

how to save

Brown-bagging your bucks

Great, you're ready to start saving some money. It really can be pain free. Here are some very smart, fairly easy ways to start stashing away some money.

STEP BY STEP:

1. Pay yourself first. This means that you need to consider your savings account as a bill you must pay before all the others. Write yourself a check every month and put it in a separate savings account, CD, or money market account (see page 13). Better still, arrange to have your paycheck deposited directly into your checking account, and then have your bank automatically transfer a certain amount into your savings account. That way you never see it— and what you don't see, you don't spend. Let's hope.

2. Keep a coin drawer. At the end of the day, put all your loose change in a drawer or jar. Don't spend it. Just let the coins accumulate. Every four months sort and count it, and deposit it at your bank. Depending on your spending habits, you can save anywhere from $200 to $400 a year.

3. Spend more wisely. Instead of buying groceries at the local store, join a discount warehouse and buy your household items in bulk. If you can buy in bulk, the prices are much lower.

4. Put instant gratification on hold. A $3 cappuccino or a $1.50 coffee? Go with the coffee and pocket the difference. Lunch with co-workers at Designer Diner vs. chicken salad from last night's leftovers? Brown-bag it and stash the savings. Paying the lawn guy $25 again? Mow the grass yourself or with your kids, and pocket some green while you're cutting it! Another $100 Saturday night dinner and a movie for two? Picnic on pizza and sparkling cider, then rent a romantic comedy. Savings? About $75. Considering a week with the family at CartoonWorld vs. camping at a state park? Borrow a tent, pack up the coolers—and save thousands of dollars!

MONEY SAVING TIPS

■ Eat breakfast at home instead of buying it on the way to work. Make your lunch and take it to work or school.

■ Swap soda for tap water at work and at home. (It will shrink your waistline, too!)

■ Eliminate trips to the vending machine during your breaks. Instead, bring a snack from home.

■ Stop with the expensive gifts—give of your time instead. Watch your brother's kids for the weekend, give a friend a homemade dinner, or create a coupon book of treats and favors for your mate.

■ Declare an embargo on new toys. Wrap up some out-of-favor toys and put them away for a few months, then take them out of storage with much fanfare, and retire another set. Swap toys with friends.

■ To compare prices and save gas and time, shop on-line. Buy only what you're looking for, and don't forget to add in shipping charges when comparing prices.

■ Trade in your pricey car, with monthly payments you can't afford, for something reliable and reasonably priced.

■ If you're tempted to buy a new gadget or piece of clothing when shopping, go home and sleep on the decision. Then see how important the new item seems in the morning.

■ Keep reading this book. It's full of ways to save money on taxes, insurance, banking, and investing.

ranking your goals

*Making a
master plan*

So you haven't saved a dime. What makes you want to start now? Chances are something costly is tapping you on the shoulder. A car. A wedding. A house. College tuition. Retirement. It's important to understand why you're saving, as your goals become the beacon you sail toward. List your top three financial goals and, more importantly, when you want to achieve them. Your time frame will greatly affect how you finance them. If you have a partner, each of you separately should list your top three goals. After you've made individual lists, get together and talk honestly about your goals. Try to agree on two or three. When you share the driving, it's easier to make the trip.

Next, draw up a master plan that outlines how much money you think you need for each goal, and when you'll need it. Divide the amount you need by the number of months remaining before you plan to spend it, so you can figure out how much to start saving each month toward each goal.

ASK THE EXPERTS

When should I start investing my savings in something a little riskier, say stocks or bonds or some mutual funds?

You shouldn't invest in stocks and bonds until you have accumulated enough savings to form a comfortable financial cushion. Then, if you were to lose part of your investment, you would not be in serious financial difficulty. The important point to remember is this: When you begin saving, don't risk your stash on anything. (See pages 68–69 to learn more about risk and reward.)

buying a house

If you're like most people, you'll have to take out a loan to buy new digs. But unlike the "bad" debt that gets racked up on credit cards, a mortgage is a loan worth taking. With each mortgage payment you own a little more house. If history is an indicator, the value of your house will increase over time. And the interest you pay on the mortgage is tax deductible, too.

How much house can you afford? Mortgage lenders will typically loan you about two and a half to three times your annual income, depending on your other debts. But don't borrow so much that you're stretched to the limit each month. Here's how mortgage lenders see it: Your projected monthly housing costs (including mortgage payments, property taxes, and insurance) shouldn't exceed 28% of your gross monthly income. (Gross is your total income before any deductions for taxes.) These costs plus your other long-term debt payments (like car loans, credit card payments, and student loans) shouldn't exceed 36% of your gross monthly income.

Aim to squirrel away about 20% of the price of the house for a down payment. If you can't muster that much, you'll have to pay for private mortgage insurance, which protects the bank in case you can't make your payments. If you can't afford the down payment but have enough income to afford monthly payments, check out government-backed loans from Fannie Mae (800) 732-6643 (**www.fanniemae.com**), or the Federal Housing Administration (800) 483-7342 (**www.hud.gov/fha**).

You'll have to save more than down-payment money. Heaped on the down payment like meatballs on spaghetti will be fees and closing costs, to the tune of about 3% to 5% of the amount you are borrowing.

HOME, HOME IN YOUR RANGE

Median price of a house in 2002: $157,700.
The median price ranges from $83,800 in sections of Kansas to over $540,000 in San Francisco.

Source: National Association of Realtors

ASK THE EXPERTS

What saves me more money: a fixed-rate mortgage or an adjustable-rate mortgage (ARM)?

That depends on how long you're staying. If you don't plan to stay in the house more than three to five or six years, you're typically better off with an ARM, as lenders tend to offer initial rates for ARMs that are a couple of percentage points lower than fixed rates. Be careful of those teasers, though, because the ARM rate escalates over time. With a fixed rate, your monthly mortgage payments stay the same for the life of the loan, even if interest rates shoot sky-high.

What are points? And am I better off buying a point or paying a higher interest rate?

A point is banktalk for one interest point. If you buy a point, you are paying one percent of your total loan up-front in order to reduce your rate of interest and, therefore, reduce your monthly payments. Most banks let you "buy" them to lower your monthly interest payment. You are not lowering your interest rate point for point, however; usually your rate will be lowered by a half or a quarter of a point. For example, if you are offered a loan at 8%, you can buy a point up front and lower your loan to 7.75%. If you plan to stay in your home for five years or more, then it makes sense to buy points because you will save money in the long run due to lower monthly mortgage payments. If you are going to be in your home for five years or less, then buying points might be a waste of money. If you decide to buy a point or two, remember this at tax time—points paid when you buy a new home are fully deductible.

60 SECONDS $ SAVINGS

Coming up short at closing time? If you're buying a home for the first time, you can withdraw up to $10,000 from your Individual Retirement Account without penalty (although you still have to pay taxes on the money). You can also hit up Mom and Dad (and Mom-in-Law and Dad-in-Law) for a gift on which you pay no taxes. All four of them can give both you and your spouse up to $11,000 —a potential windfall of $88,000! (Okay, wishful thinking...)

buying a car

Unlike buying a house, whose value increases over time, buying a new car is not an investment. The instant you drive it off the lot, your car's value drops by about 10%. For this reason, think hard about sinking your valuable savings into an expensive new car.

When you need a new set of wheels, you have to make two major decisions: to lease or to buy, and to choose new or used. If you're the type who trades in your car every couple of years, go with a lease. Here you pay a portion of what the car costs with each lease payment. At the end of the lease you return the car and owe nothing, or you can buy the car. But if you intend to keep a car for more than a few years, drive more than 15,000 miles a year, and have enough money for the down payment, buying is your best bet.

If you really want to save, buy or lease a solid used car that's two or three years old. With a used car, the down payment, monthly payments, and insurance are less than for a new car, often substantially less. If the pre-owned car is certified by the manufacturer, it will come with a warranty.

Whether you buy or lease, you can save loads if you negotiate the price. Know that the sticker price does not reflect what the car and its options really cost the dealer. A reference librarian can show you where to find out the true costs, or you can investigate on-line. Check out **www.carpoint.com**, **www.autoworld.com**, and **www.kelleybluebook.com**, among others. For a used car, check out the Kelley Blue Book (**www.kelleybluebook.com**) or the Official Used Car Guide of the National Automobile Dealer's Association (**www.nada.org**).

Once you decide which make, model, and options you like, and you learn their true costs, call around to dealers and start the bidding. Be frank about what you're doing, but don't mention rebates or trade-ins until you negotiate a final cost for the car you want. If a dealer doesn't cooperate, that dealer is out of the running.

WHEELING AND DEALING ON THE CAR LOT

Average cost of a new car: $25,800. Whether you buy or lease, it's not only car payments you have to come up with. The American Automobile Association has estimated that motorists who drive 15,000 miles a year pile on $7,363 more in car-related expenses, including insurance costs and personal property taxes.

STEP BY STEP: CAR FINANCING

1. Find out the going interest rates on new- and used-car loans in order to know the range of rates being offered. (To learn the national averages, check out www.bankrate.com.)

2. No matter who finances your car, ask for the lowest interest rate, not the lowest monthly payment.

3. Try to get a loan pre-approved before you go car shopping, so you know how much you can afford and what the terms are before you get giddy on that new-car smell and temporarily lose your good sense.

4. Go for a simple-interest loan instead of an installment loan (also called a front-end loan). With the former, you pay interest only on the remaining principal. With the latter, you pay interest on the entire principal throughout the term of the loan. (In other words, with an installment loan, even if you have paid off $8,000 of a $15,000 loan, you keep paying interest on the entire $15,000!)

5. If you're a homeowner, you can take out a home equity loan to finance your car. Generally the rate is not only cheaper, but also the interest you pay is usually tax deductible.

LEASING LINGO

Capitalized cost—the selling price, which you want to drive down as low as you can.
Residual value—how much the car will be worth at the end of the lease (you negotiate this at the time of the lease). The difference between the capitalized cost and the residual value, plus the finance charge, is what you pay to lease the car each month.

having a baby

A joyful bundle of expenses

Congratulations, you're going to have a baby! But along with those adorable smiles and coos comes a steady stream of bills. Even before the baby arrives, there's the obstetrician's bill, which ranges from $2,000 to $6,000. Then there's the hospital bill and the pediatrician's bill. By the time your bundle is ready to go home, you'll be handed bills of around $8,000. If you are even thinking of having a baby, check your health insurance policy to see exactly what it does and doesn't cover.

Next step: bringing your darling home. Many people mistakenly assume a tiny human being does not eat much or need many things. But the U.S. Department of Agriculture (USDA) estimates that as of 1999 the average family spends about $9,420 a year to raise each child—about $160,140 from birth to age 17. And that doesn't include paying for college!

About a third of that USDA estimate goes for the bigger house or apartment you need. But there's still another $6,280 in other special expenses: a baby uses about $1,000 of infant food each year, $450 in clothing, $560 in health care, and $1,200 in medical care, diapers, and supplies.

What to do? Plan and save for the expense of having children before you have them. You may need to scale back elsewhere to accommodate the baby's needs. Now is a good time to rethink your monthly expenses. Where can you cut back? Maybe forgo expensive entertainment items or put off the vacation. Take some time and go through the baby fiscal checklist on the next page.

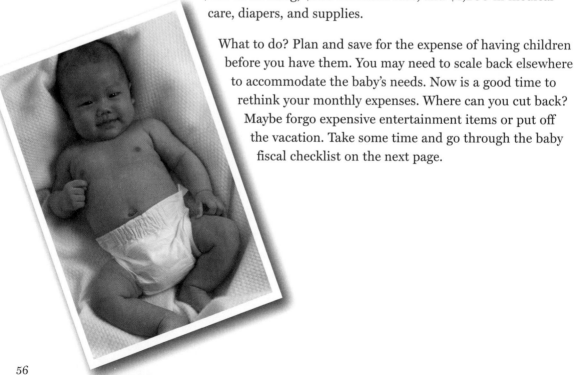

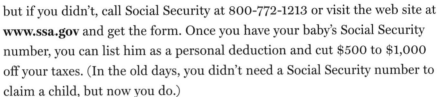

STEP BY STEP: NEW BABY BASICS CHECKLIST

1. Get your child a social security number. Usually you fill out the form in the hospital, but if you didn't, call Social Security at 800-772-1213 or visit the web site at **www.ssa.gov** and get the form. Once you have your baby's Social Security number, you can list him as a personal deduction and cut $500 to $1,000 off your taxes. (In the old days, you didn't need a Social Security number to claim a child, but now you do.)

2. Review your insurance. Before kids it was just you and your spouse. Now you need to factor in the needs of a child for at least 18 years, more if you want to include college. Make sure you have enough life insurance (see page 110) to cover baby's needs as well as your spouse's. Review your disability policy (see page 114) and increase it if necessary.

3. Check your will. If you don't have a will, draft one (see page 172 to learn how). If you have a will, revise it to include your new heir. This is grim, but necessary: You need to name legal guardians for all your minor children, should you and your spouse die unexpectedly.

4. Review your investment beneficiaries. Check all investments that require you to list beneficiaries, such as your life insurance and retirement plans. Prior to having a baby, you probably listed your spouse as your primary **beneficiary** (the person who gets the proceeds from your investments should you die). It's smart to have your children listed as secondary beneficiaries to make sure they get the money in the event you and your spouse pass away simultaneously.

5. Plan your tax strategy. Review the exciting world of taxes and children on page 167.

6. Think way ahead to college. Start a college fund early. If you can muster the strength and discretionary income to open an account now, the wonder of compounding interest will reward you later. See page 59 for types of funds.

7. Organize your files along with all those baby albums. And keep a financial file for baby, so that vital financial papers can be found quickly if there is an emergency,

tackling tuition

Didn't get around to starting the college fund when
Sweet Pea was in diapers, and here she is taking her SAT exams? Don't sweat it. Most people can't save enough to pay the whole tuition tab. If you don't have a reasonably high salary, your child may qualify for aid and grants. If you do make enough, but have other expenses, you and your college-bound child can always take out loans.

You won't be alone. Americans borrow more than *$65 billion a year* to pay tuition. But paying for college—even if you have to borrow money to do it—is without doubt a good investment. Based on history, there is a payback: college grads earn twice the annual salary of high school grads!

The best way to save for college costs is—surprise—to spend within your means. To save many thousands of dollars, consider the fact that there are many excellent state universities as well as community colleges with fine courses available. Consider having your child enroll in a community college for a semester or a year or two, then transfer to a more prestigious school for the last two years and the diploma. Or trim off the number of semesters you have to pay at an expensive college by supplementing it with credits taken at a less expensive college. (Just make sure the tuition credits are transferable.)

HOW MUCH COLLEGE COSTS

Projected average annual cost of a
private college, including room and board:

2003: $25,586	2008: $32,656
2004: $26,866	2009: $34,288
2005: $28,209	2010: $36,003
2006: $29,620	2011: $37,803
2007: $31,100	2012: $39,693

Add about a third if your child sets her sights
on ivy league schools, and subtract about a
third for State U and other public schools.

Source: The Princeton Review

ASK THE EXPERTS

My son needs financial aid to pay for his college. How will I know if we qualify for it?

The answer lies not with the whim of the school's financial aid officer, but with a process approved by Congress. Most colleges ask you to fill out the Free Application for Federal Student Aid. (Get it from the guidance counselor or on-line at **www.fafsa.ed.gov**.) Other colleges request the Financial Aid Form. Essentially, you add up your (and your child's) income and any non-retirement financial accounts you have (such as investments), and a formula calculates the magic number you are expected to pay: the Estimated Family Contribution (EFC). It's important to note that money you have saved in retirement accounts such as IRAs and Keoghs are NOT included, so don't forgo investing in your retirement because you think it will hurt your child's chance of getting financial aid. Here's something interesting: the EFC is the same regardless of the price of the college. Remember, aid doesn't mean free money. More often than not, it refers to work-study programs or loans that you or your child must pay back.

Are there any savings plans that help me save for my child's college education?

There are two types of plans to choose from. In a Coverdell Education IRA you can contribute up to $2,000 a year per child; money you earn on that investment is tax free if it's ultimately used toward college. The second plan is offered by individual states. It's called the 529 plan. Here you can save up to ten times more ($200,000) in a state-managed fund. The money you earn compounds tax-free and is generally not taxed when it's withdrawn either. The money can be used to pay for the college of your choice. Check out **www.savingforcollege.com** or **www.collegesavings.org** for more information about saving for college.

now what do I do?

Answers to common questions

I want to pay for my own wedding. How much will it cost?

Weddings are expensive. Engraved invitations alone can cost $500. Then there's the dress, renting a room, restaurant, or hall, music, flowers, food and liquor, photography. It all adds up. The average wedding is now nearly $20,000. And then there's the honeymoon. You don't want to start a marriage burdened with debt from the wedding. That's why it's important to plan and save as far in advance of the big day as you possibly can.

My wife and I are getting divorced. How much will it cost?

The cost of an uncontested divorce (where both parties mutually agree to a divorce) is about $500 (that's the average fee most lawyers charge to file an uncontested divorce with the courts). The average cost of a contested divorce is $20,000 if the couple has no children, and $40,000 if they do. To save money, see a mediator who will try to work out a deal that is mutually acceptable to both of you. A mediator is a lot cheaper than hiring two divorce lawyers. That said, make sure you have your lawyer check the mediation agreement to ensure you are getting what you are entitled to receive.

Can I pay for my child's college eduction with IRA money?

Yes. Although you will be taxed, withdrawals from traditional or Roth IRAs are not subject to additional penalties if they're used to pay for college expenses. For traditional IRAs you will be taxed on the entire amount of the withdrawal; for the Roth you will only be taxed on any earnings you've accumulated.

How can I find the lowest rates for a mortgage?

Start calling banks, mortgage companies, and mortgage brokers, and searching on-line (**www.bankrate.com**, **www.loanworks.com**, and **www.eloan.com** are good places to start). To compare the real cost of a loan from lender to lender, ask for the APR, or annual percentage rate. This includes interest plus fees and points (see page 53). Don't be afraid to ask your local banker if she can match or beat a competitor's rates, or at least waive fees or point charges.

HELPFUL RESOURCES

WEB ADDRESSES	BOOKS
www.money.cnn.com www.homeadvisor.msn.com www.mortgage.quicken.com www.bankrate.com www.ssa.gov	**10 Steps to Financial Success: A Beginner's Guide to Saving and Investing** by W. Patrick Naylor **The Complete Tightwad Gazette** by Amy Dacyczn **Slash Your Debt, Save Money, and Secure Your Future** by Gerri Detweiler, Marc Eisenson, and Nancy Castleman

Investing

4

INVESTING

"The incredible thing about investing is that you don't actually have to save up all the money you need to reach your goal."

investing basics

The rules of the game

You've started to save a bit and are now ready to think about investing it. Congratulations! You are on your way to achieving your financial goals. The great news about investing is that you don't actually have to save up all the money you need to reach your goals. Sometimes you don't even have to come close. All you have to do is put your savings in investments that are capable of significant appreciation, yet behave with acceptable predictability. Okay, yes, that is a bit easier said than done.

Two things you need to consider before you invest a dime:

1. How much money you want your investment to earn over time—this is called its **return**.

2. How much you are willing to **risk**—the possibility of not earning a dime or even losing your entire investment. Here's a tough investment rule of thumb: The higher the return you want, the higher the risk you need to be willing to take.

Two more things you need to consider: **taxes** and **inflation**. If you think of investing as a game, then these two guys are the opponents you need to beat. Why? Because the government is going to tax any money you make. Inflation will take a bite out of your return, too. **Inflation** is the rise in prices of goods and services. It usually goes up every year. Some years it increases a little, some years a lot. The point is that, over time, it can decrease the real value of your money. Smart investors factor in taxes and inflation. You can too. Read on and learn how.

Inflation Rates over the Years

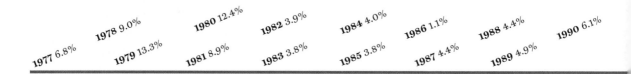

1977 6.8% 1978 9.0% 1979 13.3% 1980 12.4% 1981 8.9% 1982 3.9% 1983 3.8% 1984 4.0% 1985 3.8% 1986 1.1% 1987 4.4% 1988 4.4% 1989 4.9% 1990 6.1%

THE PERILS OF INFLATION

Inflation is what happens when prices go up. (The difference between how much a car cost 10 years ago and today is due mostly to inflation.) Historically, inflation eats up about 3% a year from the value of your savings. That's why you never want to stash greenbacks under the mattress. In other words, if inflation follows its historic path, the dollar you hid under the mattress today will buy only 97 cents worth of goods next year. The following year, your 97 cents buys 3% less, and so on. In time, your hard-saved money will be worth less than half of its value. Or look at it this way: thanks to inflation, $1,000 put under the mattress today will be worth $859 in five years, $737 in 10 years. Ouch! But there is a remedy: invest your money so it earns a rate of return that is higher than inflation.

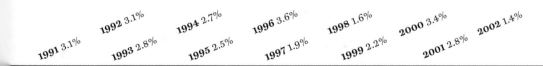

1991 3.1% 1992 3.1% 1993 2.8% 1994 2.7% 1995 2.5% 1996 3.6% 1997 1.9% 1998 1.6% 1999 2.2% 2000 3.4% 2001 2.8% 2002 1.4%

short- and long-term

It's about time

If all you need to do to invest is seek out higher returns, why do so many investors fail? Often the answer has to do with time. How long do you have to wait for your investments to pay off? In other words, when do you plan to reach your financial goals? Financial experts divide it this way: If you want to buy a car or house in the next one to four years, that's a short-term goal. If you want to invest for a child's college education five to ten years from now, that's a mid-term goal. Finally, if you are investing for anything that's ten or more years away, say retirement or a second home, that's considered a long-term goal.

To a great extent, your time frame determines your investing style and choices. The less time you have, the more conservative you need to be. Why? Because you can't risk blowing your money on a risky investment if you need it in one year's time to buy a car. If you are investing to achieve long-term goals, you can invest more aggressively, meaning you can put your money in high-risk, high-return investments. Should they tumble, and chances are they will from time to time, you can ride it out.

Unfortunately, in their haste to accumulate wealth, many so-called investors behave like speculators: They rush into and out of different investments, chasing a pot of gold. But given enough time, an investment vehicle can right its course, or an investor can change vehicles in order to continue on the right path. Over time, returns compound on each other until the investment takes on a life of its own. That's why it's important to invest as soon as you can. Accumulation takes time.

INVESTING OVER TIME

Consider this: If you put $3,000 in a savings account that pays 3% interest, you will earn $91.25 in a year. But what if you put it in a different vehicle, one that delivers a higher return? Look at what could happen to that account over time. (Remember, this is without putting in another dime.)

	Savings Account 3%	Money Market 5.5%	Stock Fund 12%
1 year	3,091	3,169	3,380
3 years	3,282	3,537	4,292
10 years	4,048	5,193	9,901
14 years	4,564	6,468	15,963
15 years	4,702	6,833	17,987
20 years	5,462	8,990	32,678
22 years	5,800	10,033	41,492
27 years	6,737	13,200	75,378
30 years	7,371	15,562	107,849

piloting risk and return

Smooth sailing through stormy seas

Here's a question: How much risk can you handle?

In other words, how comfortable are you with taking risks? For instance, suppose you want to take a short trip—like a weekend at the shore—and suddenly the weatherman predicts a hurricane. Chances are, the risk of danger would outweigh the benefits (or return) the getaway might bring.

But what if the trip is longer? Say, for example, you're planning to take a six-month sabbatical to travel around the world. Would you cancel the trip because there may be a hurricane along the way? Or would you go anyway, accepting that you might have to weather a storm or two en route?

This is the quandary you face as an investor: Are the potential rewards worth the risks you must brave along the way? Risk is the possibility that an investment will not perform according to expectation, resulting in less money in the kitty than you had anticipated. The best way to combat risk is with research. Take a look at an investment's performance over time. Did it perform better in some years than in others? Were there identifiable reasons for the lows, say a sudden rise in oil prices that offset profits? The retirement of an effective company chairman? Now consider the present and the future. What is this investment's potential? Have you found information on how and when it might make money? What problems could it encounter along the way? If you can't answer all of these questions, you are not alone. No one can predict the future. Hence the need to take risks.

It is this riskiness that drives returns: People want to be rewarded more handsomely for investing in less predictable investments. At the same time, they can suffer greater consequences if the investment crashes. For example, a savings account, which is about the safest place to park your money, returns just a couple of percent in interest. But over time, stocks, which may seem to skyrocket one minute and plunge the next, return an average of 12% a year.

ASK YOURSELF

How can I figure out what kind of risk I can handle before I invest?

Your comfort level depends on your individual circumstances, including your age, how much time you have to meet your goal, how much extra money you have on hand, the size of your portfolio, your income, and how jittery you get in the face of volatility. That said, the only real way to know is to take a few small steps and see how you fare. As one wise investor put it: If you're not sleeping at night because you're worrying about your investments, then sell them. It's not worth it.

Once I understand the risks, how aggressive should my investments be?

It depends on when you need the money. The more time you have to meet your goal, the more aggressive you can be because if your investment struggles, you have time to recover. If you need your money soon, though (say within a few years), and you have no cushion to fall back on, stay away from the riskier investments because you don't want to have to cash in when prices are down.

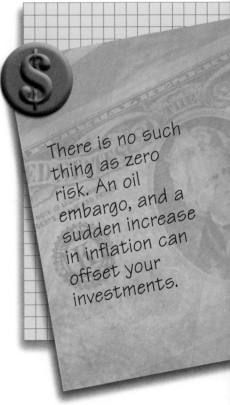

There is no such thing as zero risk. An oil embargo, and a sudden increase in inflation can offset your investments.

investing for your future

When it's good to say "uncle"

Now that you understand how time, risk, and return work together, you can get serious about investing. To start, select your most important short-, mid-, and long-term goals. Now consider the amount of money you can save each month. Think of it as a pie and cut it into three pieces, with the largest piece going toward your most important goal. For example, if you can save $325 a month, you might put $150 toward retirement (number one goal, long-term); $100 into a house down payment fund (number two goal, mid-term); and $75 for your child's college fund (number three, short-term). Next take a calculator and figure out how much money you need to earn to meet your time frame. The difference between what you have now and what you will need in the future is the amount you need to sock away and earn on your investments.

But wait. Before you sink a dime into anything, don't forget to factor in taxes. Smart investors look for tax-deferred investments to reduce their annual tax bill. One of the easiest, smartest investments around may be available at the company you work for. It's known as a 401(k), or a 403(b) if you work for a non-profit organization. If you are self-employed, you can open a SEP IRA (see page 71). All of these plans let you invest money and defer paying taxes on the interest until you retire, when you are most likely be in a lower tax bracket because you won't be working. This means you can't access the money until age 59½ without a penalty. For more on retirement saving plans, see pages 152-153; for other tax-saving strategies, see pages 144-145.

TAX-DEFERRED SAVING PLANS

Traditional IRA Short for Individual Retirement Account, it lets you put away up to $3,000 a year in essentially any investment you want and not pay taxes on what you earn until you take it out after age 59½. And you get to deduct that $3,000 from your gross income, which reduces your income taxes. There are some stipulations: you can't get the initial tax deduction if you earn more than $44,000 as a single person or $64,000 if you are married and if either you or your spouse's employer has a 401(k) plan.

Roth IRA It's an IRA available to people who make less than $95,000 if single; $150,000 if married. The bad news is that there is no up-front deduction; the good news is that whatever you earn is tax-free when you withdraw it after the age of 59½. (See page 59 for information on the Education IRA which is similar to a Roth, but can be used only to pay for college.)

SEP IRA Short for "Simplified Employee Pension," a SEP is a savings plan for self-employed people. It lets you put in pre-tax income up to 20% of your business' net earnings, up to $200,000. The earnings you make on your SEP IRA investments are tax-deferred until you withdraw them after age 59½.

401(k) This is a savings plan sponsored by employers for their employees. It lets them invest pre-tax dollars in various mutual funds that the company selects. To encourage saving, some companies contribute to each employee's 401(k) account an amount equal to what the employee sets aside. This extremely generous benefit is known as "corporate matching." The money earned in a 401(k) is tax-deferred until it's withdrawn at retirement, usually at age 65. (See page 156 for more information.)

diversify

Why not to put all your nest eggs in one little basket

You're doing great. You've figured out how time, risk, and return work together. And you've realized how smart it is to save in your company's 401(k). Fabulous. Now you are ready to get serious about investing the rest of your savings. What's left to do? Determine how best to meet your financial goals. To do this, consider the rate of return you need to earn. Now here's where it gets a little dicey. Why? Because if you put all of your money in one investment, say one particular stock, you run a greater risk of losing money than if you spread your risk among different investments. This principle is called **diversification**. Or in other words, don't put all your eggs in one basket. In chapter 5, you can read about different types of investments from which you can choose to help spread your risk.

FIRST PERSON DISASTER STORY

All in One Basket

I had worked for the same company for 17 years. They had great benefits. One of them was a 401(k). There were three or four mutual funds to choose from and then a fund of just the company stock. I put all my money in that one because it had the highest returns. Our company was growing like gangbusters! I also decided to buy some of the stock as an investment. For the first 15 years, my 401(k) soared, as did the stock price. But then the chairman died suddenly and a new CEO took over and the stock started slipping. I didn't change my 401(k) allocation, even though I could have. I just felt the company would come around. It didn't. Before I knew it, the stock was way down. By the time I was ready to retire, my 401(k) was worth about as much as when I had started 17 years before. My mother always said not to put all your eggs in one basket. I should have listened.

Barbara C., Bedford, New York

INVESTMENT STRATEGIES

Here are some hypothetical examples of diversification to give you a feel for risk and return. Generally, the higher the amount you have in stocks, the greater your risk. The question to ask yourself is how well you can emotionally and financially weather the good and bad years. Note: those minus signs mean loss!

Low risk, low return

20% money markets
50% bonds
30% stocks
Best year return: 22%
Worst year return: -5%

Medium risk, medium return

20% money markets
30% bonds
50% stocks
Best year return: 26%
Worst year return: -14%

High risk, high return

10% money markets
20% bonds
70% stocks
Best year return: 30%
Worst year return: -18%

financial planners

Mapmaker, mapmaker, make me a map

Some people feel more comfortable consulting a financial planner. What can a financial planner do for you? A planner may review your tax returns, insurance policies, retirement plan, budget, savings, and investments. She can tell you whether or not your financial goals are reachable and if your savings plan is on the right course. If you're not comfortable devising your own investing strategy, she can help you map out a plan, suggest the best routes to reach your goals, and coordinate all that you need to get there. Think of planners as money consultants. Their job is to look out for your money's best interests, not to sell you stuff. You should pay a planner for her time, either an hourly rate or a flat fee. They are called fee-only planners, and they have no financial incentive to recommend one investment over another.

You might think the government regulates financial planners, but this isn't the case at all. In fact, anybody can hang out a shingle and call herself a financial planner. That's why it's important to check the planner's credentials before you sign up.

To shop for a planner, ask for referrals from friends, colleagues, or family members whose income is in the same range as yours. To find a fee-only planner, call the National Association of Personal Financial Advisors at (888) FEE-ONLY, or go on-line to www.napfa.org.

QUESTIONS TO ASK A FINANCIAL PLANNER

■ How long have you been in practice and what types of clients do you serve?
Look for someone with clients whose income level, risk tolerance, and investment goals are like yours.

■ Do you sell financial products? How are you connected with the companies whose products you sell?

■ How often will you monitor the progress toward my goals? Every month? Every six months? Once a year?

■ How much do you charge? Who pays these fees?
Don't be embarrassed. This is a standard question to ask planners. You may be required to pay the fees, if it's a fee-only planner; otherwise the fees are paid by the various companies whose products the planner sells.

■ What's your area of expertise? What qualifies you as a specialist? What licenses do you hold? How do you stay current in the field?

■ What professional organizations do you belong to?
Ask for the phone numbers of the organizations and contact them to see if the planner is a member in good standing.

■ Do you have any clients I can talk to about their experiences working with you?

WHAT ARE THEIR QUALIFICATIONS

What a financial planner's credentials mean:

CFP: Certified Financial Planner. They've passed tests covering a wide range of financial areas, from taxes to insurance.

CLU: Chartered Life Underwriter. They've passed tests about life insurance planning.

CPA: They've passed rigorous tests about accounting and taxes.

CFA: Certified Financial Analyst. They've passed a series of in-depth tests about investing.

now what do I do?

Answers to common questions

I've been putting money in the 401(k) plan at work and my employer matches it. But now I have this sudden debt to pay off. Should I stop contributing to my 401(k) and divert the money to pay off the debt?

No. While paying off debt should always be a top priority, it might not be in this case. When you make money decisions, take the route that provides you the most for your money. While reducing credit card debt is a great "investment" if it reduces future interest expense of 18% or more, it pales in comparison to an immediate return of 100%. That's what you are "earning" on your money if you invest in a 401(k) and your employer matches the amount—dollar for dollar. Even if they only match 50 cents or 25 cents on the dollar, that's an immediate 50% or 25% return!

I want to meet with a financial planner, but I really have very little savings, and I don't earn tons of money. Do all financial planners focus on the super-wealthy?

Most—but not all. The Garrett Planning Network is a group of financial advisors who are committed to providing independent, objective financial advice to average consumers. All of their advisors work on a fee-only basis, and charge anywhere from $100 to $200 per hour. Contact them at (913) 236-4222, or visit them on-line at **www.GarrettPlanningNetwork.com**.

I don't retire for another 15 or so years, but I'm nervous about investing in the stock market—why should I invest in something that can be so turbulent?

It's certainly understandable why investing in the stock market could be disconcerting. Keep in mind, though, that if you have a long time before you need the money, you will probably be better off staying invested and letting it ride rather than sitting on the sidelines and trying to figure out market fluctuations. If you're really nervous, consider dollar cost averaging (see page 99), which allows you to invest small amounts each month. That way you won't have to predict the future market movements.

What exactly will a financial planner do for me?

If it's your first visit to a planner, think of it as your very first trip to the doctor. He should start by asking you questions. A doctor might start with, "What are your complaints?" A planner may ask what prompted your visit. If you're there only to address an emergency (such as out of control debt, or enrollment decisions with a deadline), the planner will help you with your problem. Once addressed, if you want a complete fiscal physical, the planner will ask more questions, and may ask to see your tax returns, investment statements, and other financial documents that will help her understand your big financial picture. Besides the concrete stuff, the planner should ask some touchy-feely questions to get a handle on your goals, hopes, dreams, and fears, regarding your money. Once they understand where you are, and where you want to go, they'll make recommendations about the best way to get there. Depending on your needs, this might mean helping you with a budget, suggesting changes to your investments, or calculating the amount of insurance you need.

HELPFUL RESOURCES

WEB SITES	BOOKS
www.investoreducation.org Provides a wide variety of excellent resources including investing basics, help choosing an advisor, and basic information about on-line investing.	**You and Your 401(k): How to Manage Your 401(k) for Maximum Returns** by Julie Jason
	Got Money? by Jeff Wuorio
www.invest-faq.com The Investment FAQ is a collection of frequently asked questions and answers about investments and personal finance, including stocks, bonds, options, discount brokers, information sources, retirement plans, life insurance, etc.	**The First Book of Investing** by Samuel Case
	The Truth About Money by Ric Edelman

Stocks, bonds, mutual funds

" Every year give
your portfolio a
physical to make
sure it's still on
track to meet your
goals and that all
parts are healthy. "

investments 101

*What to put in
your portfolio*

Your financial house is in order and you are ready to
invest. You know your goals (see page 50) so you know your
investing time frame. Great. Wonderful. You're good to go. It's
time to create your own financial **portfolio**—a diverse collection
of financial products. Here's a brief overview of your choices.
Detailed information on why, how, and where to buy them follows
in these pages.

Stocks are shares of ownership in a company that
give you a claim on the company's earnings. They
"share" their earnings with you in the form of **dividends**. They also "share" the risk of making or
losing money, which is reflected in the rise or fall
of the stock price. Because a share of stock means
you own a tiny piece of the company, it is called
equity. As a company becomes more valuable, its
stock becomes more attractive and the price
should rise.

Bonds are IOUs from a company or the government. In a sense you are loaning money to the
company and it is promising to pay back what
you lent them, plus interest. Bonds are also called
fixed income vehicles because the interest they
pay never varies. Although not as glamorous as
stocks, bonds provide stability when stocks are rocking. (You'll
learn why in a couple of pages.)

Mutual funds are a mix of stocks and bonds, as well as other good-
ies or **assets** such as money markets or real estate. A professional
money manager runs the fund, buying and selling stocks and bonds
to enrich the fund's value. When you buy shares of a mutual fund,
you are buying a piece of all those investments. If you are brand
new to investing, start with mutual funds. More on how later.

ASK THE EXPERTS

Do I have to pay taxes on the money I make on investments?

You bet you do. When you sell a bond or your shares of stocks or mutual funds for more than you paid for them, it's called a capital gain. And yes, you have to pay taxes on it. If your gain happened within one year, or short term, it's considered regular income and taxed at whatever income tax rate you qualify for—probably from 27% to 35%. If you hold an investment for a year or more and then sell it at a profit, it's called a long-term gain and is taxed at either 20% or 10% depending on your total income. If you decide to sell at a lower price than you paid, this is called a capital loss. Happily, you get to deduct up to $3,000 of that loss from your taxes (see page 145). Oh, yes, and any interest or dividends you receive are also taxed at your regular rate. And capital gains, dividends, and interest are generally taxed by the state you live in, too. Because taxes can figure so prominently in how well your investments do, smart investors consider the tax consequences before they invest. For more on investment strategies, see page 144.

Are any investments tax free?

Yes. The interest you earn on municipal bonds is usually tax free from federal income taxes. These are bonds issued by a state or local municipality to help finance public works projects—construction such as building hospitals or schools. More about those on page 96.

what's a stock?

*Own a piece of
your favorite
company*

You can own a piece of any public company you want, say the one that made the car you drive or the clothes you wear or the soap you do the dishes with. All you have to do is buy stock in the company.

Here's how stocks are born: When the owners of a private company need to raise lots of money to expand their business, they can **go public**—in other words, they sell ownership in the company to outsiders. Investors buy pieces, or **shares of stock**, of the company, and become part owners. This first-time sale of stock is called an **Initial Public Offering** or **IPO**. The sale takes place on a stock exchange; the choice of exchange is determined by the size of the company and the offering. Once the company goes public, it is listed on the exchange and its stock can be traded—bought and sold—every day by the public. (And yes, if the company wants to raise money again, it can issue more stock.)

As the company becomes more profitable and its earnings increase, its stock price should rise. So, too, should the amount of the **dividends** it pays to investors. (The amount of the dividend is determined by the company's board of directors at quarterly meetings.) Think of the dividend as a cash bonus.

In a perfect world, all stock prices would rise steadily. Alas, all sorts of things can happen to affect the price of a stock: changes in interest rates, rising or falling inflation, amendments to the tax code, changes in production, increased competition, fluctuations of the dollar overseas. You name it.

The rise and fall (called **volatility** in investor-speak) of stock prices is part of the risk of investing in stocks. Why bother with such risk? Because of the tantalizing returns. Historically, stocks have done very well indeed, typically returning about 12% a year since 1950.

ASK YOURSELF

What's the least risky stock to invest in?

Traditionally, utility stocks (shares of companies that provide electricity) tend to offer dividends as well as slow and steady growth. This means that the price of the stock does not rise and fall very much. They are generally the least risky of all stocks.

How do I tell whether or not a stock is good?

Before buying stock in a company, you need to check out a little bit about the company and its performance over the last 5 to 10 years. Value Line and Standard & Poor's publish reputable stock guides to consult. The following information is listed:

Dividends. Look for payment of rising dividends over the last 10 years.

Annual earnings. How much money is the company making? You want to see improvement in at least 5 out of the last 10 years.

The stock's price-to-earnings (P/E) ratio. This number reflects the price of one share of stock divided by the company's net earnings during the past four quarters. The average P/E for stocks in late 2002 is about 21. Anything over that means investors think the company is growing very fast and is positioned to make a lot of money. However, it can also mean that the stock price is overvalued.

Stock rating. If figuring out all of these details seems too much, then let experts do the math for you. Two top stock rating firms, Standard & Poor's and Value Line, track all the major stocks and offer succinct analysis.

STOCK RESEARCH

To find out about the financial health of a company and its stock, you can check out two key sources.

Standard & Poor's stock guide. S&P's tracks hundreds of companies and reports on each one, listing all the key information. The book is in most local libraries, as well as on-line at **www.businessweek.com/ investor/**

Value Line's stock guides. Similar information to that in the Standard & Poor's guide. VL's guide is also available at most libraries, or look for it on-line at **www.valueline.com**

the stock markets

Where stocks are listed

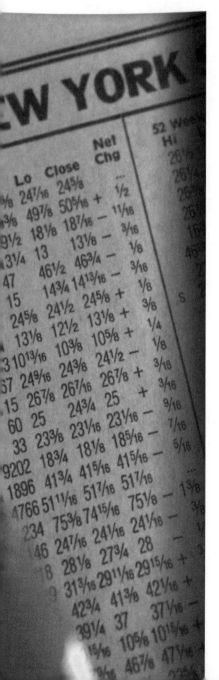

Stock markets are just that—markets where you can buy and sell stocks. In the financial world these markets are called **exchanges**. (That makes sense considering how much exchanging of stock goes on each day—about one billion shares a day!) There are two basic types of exchanges: **listed** and **NASDAQ**. The only real difference is how the stocks are sold. At **listed** exchanges, the companies are "listed" on a big board (it's now an electronic board), and salespeople called **specialists** are allowed by the exchange to handle a specific stock. Their job is to ensure an orderly market in their particular stock by matching buyers with sellers. Who are the buyers and sellers? Licensed stockbrokers who are buying and selling stock based on the requests of their clients—like you. (Learn more about stockbrokers on page 86.) The New York Stock Exchange (NYSE) has more than 2,800 companies listed on its "big board." About 480 specialists work on its trading floor, "specializing" in an average of about four stocks each. (There are other regional listed exchanges around the country.)

At the NASDAQ stock market, there aren't any specialists on the trading floor. In fact, there's no floor at all, as all transactions occur electronically via computers and phones. Think of it as the electronic stock market. Instead of specialists, they have **market makers** who are obligated to keep order in the stocks they choose. While some stocks may have as many as 380 market makers, the average is 11. The NASDAQ lists the stocks of more than 4,800 companies.

ASK THE EXPERTS

I understand there are some stocks I can buy right from the company. How do I do this?

More than 900 **blue-chip** companies (nationally known companies that have a long history of profitability) that pay dividends allow you to buy stocks directly from them through a **Dividend Reinvestment Plan**, or **DRIP**. To do so, you must already own at least one share, then any dividends it earns are automatically reinvested to purchase more shares. Some companies even let you send in extra money for additional shares. The beautiful thing about DRIPs is that you can buy shares, even one or two at a time, without paying a commission each time you buy—an economical, painless, disciplined method of building up your nest egg with stocks you plan on holding for the long-term.

What are penny stocks?

These are stocks that sometimes sell for pennies (hence the name). They are traded on something called the **OTC** or the **Over-the-Counter Exchange**. These stocks usually have uneven track records, which makes investing in them very risky. They are also referred to as "pink sheet" stocks.

What's the difference between a bull and a bear market?

A **bull market** is when stock prices are increasing overall; a **bear market** is when stocks prices are declining. These names arose from the observation that when a bull strikes he butts upward with his horns while a bear swipes down with his paws.

stockbrokers

Want some help finding value in the markets?

Contrary to what many TV ads lead you to believe, you can't buy or sell a stock by yourself, even if you make your own investment decisions and invest on-line. You need somebody with a license to sell stock to execute your trades. That somebody is called a **stockbroker**. (Stockbrokers also sell bonds, mutual funds, and other types of investments.) There are two types of brokers: full-service and discount.

A full-service broker works for an established brokerage house. When you go to his office, he should review your financial situation, give you tips on how to improve it, share the company's research with you, execute your trades, and advise you against doing anything foolish. With a full-service broker, you don't have to do anything but tell him what your financial goals are. For this broad range of services, he will charge a high commission on every trade he makes for you, anywhere from .5% to 2% on each trade. (That goes for buying as well as selling.)

If you want to direct your own trades without the help of advice, you can use a **discount broker** to simply make the trade for you. His commissions typically run from $10 to $30 per trade. Most discount brokers work on-line or by phone.

ASK THE EXPERTS

How do I find a good full-service stockbroker?

Ask for referrals from your accountant first. Check with your local chamber of commerce to see if any stockbrokers are members. Once you've found a few candidates, call and interview them. Ask them hypothetical questions: for example, if you had $10,000 to invest for your 10-year-old's college tuition, how would you invest it? If possible, meet with each candidate to see whose style matches yours. Some brokers are great stock pickers, but shy away from financial planning. Others are very knowledgeable about mutual funds, but give little advice on individual stocks.

A stock I owned started to go down in price. I told my broker to sell it. When I got the statement, I saw it was sold at far less than I expected. What happened?

When you put in an order to sell stock, you need to be specific about how you want it handled. If you say you want it sold without putting a specific price limit on it, your broker will sell it that business day and take whatever deal he can get. He can't predict the stock's selling price. If the stock is falling, there may be few buyers so the price may be much lower than expected. If you want it sold at a specific price, you need to give a limit order and state the price.

My broker keeps calling and asking me to trade this and that stock. I just want to hold my stock. All this activity makes me nervous.

Excessive trading is called **churning** in the financial world. Unscrupulous brokers do it to beef up their commissions. It is illegal. If you feel your broker is too aggressive with your account, immediately contact his or her supervisor and report it.

reading stock tables

All the fine print explained

Open the newspaper to check on your stocks and you may need an interpreter for all those abbreviations and symbols. Here's the translation of a hypothetical stock quote—or snapshot of the day's activity—from Buy Our Stellar Stuff, Inc. (BOSS). Transactions at exchanges in the United States are listed in dollars; in other countries, they are listed in that nation's currency.

Stock. The stock's symbol on the exchange is also called its ticker symbol. If the symbol contains three or fewer letters, the stock trades on the New York or American stock exchanges. A four-letter symbol

| 52-Week | | | | | | | | | | |
Stock	High	Low	Div	%	P/E	100s	High	Low	Last	Change
BOSS	49.56	26.38	.20	0.7	19	101175	28.81	27.06	28.00	+1.06

indicates it's a NASDAQ stock, and five letters ending in X usually denotes a mutual fund.

High/Low. The most and the least paid for the stock during the past 52 weeks of trading (in dollars).

Div or Dividend. How much money the company returns to stockholders annually for each share they own (in dollars).

Yield. The dividend divided by the stock's closing price, expressed as a percentage.

P/E or Price-to-Earnings Ratio. This number reflects the price of one share of stock divided by the company's net earnings during the past four quarters. If there's no P/E, it means the company has no earnings yet. (This is not uncommon with new companies.)

100s or Volume/Sales. The number of shares exchanged during the trading day (reported in hundreds).

High. The most paid for one share during the trading day.

Low. The least paid for one share of stock during the trading day.

Last or Close. The last price at the end of the trading day.

Change. How much the price changed above or below the previous day's close.

ASK THE EXPERTS

How do I measure how my stock is doing?

You compare it to other stocks. Ah, but which ones? That's where the S&P 500—a collection of 500 stocks chosen by Standard & Poor's—comes in. Every day, it combines the rise and fall of those stock prices to get an average return for the day. If you read that the S&P 500 is up, it usually means that the stock market is up overall.

Another stock measurement is the Dow Jones Industrial Average, which averages the stock prices of 30 large companies. Many investors feel the Dow Jones is a good way to measure how the stock market is doing. If "the Dow" is up, then usually so is the market.

Another important stock index is the NASDAQ Composite Index. If it's up, usually so is the NASDAQ (see page 84).

FIRST PERSON   DISASTER STORY

Hot Tip Gone Cold

I got a great tip from my Uncle Marty who works as a computer analyst. He told me about a computer company called Hot.com that was going public and was a sure winner. I'd never invested before, but if Marty said it was a winner, well, he ought to know. I put my entire IRA money in it, all $5,000. When it opened the first day, I bought it at $23. It continued to do well and got up to $55. I was thrilled, ecstatic. Who knew investing could be so easy? Then something happened. Over the weekend, Hot.com lost one of its backers, and the stock dropped to $46. Then another backer fell away. Then their first earnings came out and they were much lower than anyone had anticipated and more backers left. In one day the stock fell from $35 to $18. But I still held on. I was sure it would turn around. I mean if it could go as high as $55 it could get back up there. I held on at $10, even at $4. I knew it was over, but I couldn't bring myself to admit I was wrong. Then it hit $2. Call me stupid and stubborn because I still thought it would come back. Hot.com filed for bankruptcy.

Stanley Z., New Paltz, New York

financial Web sites

All your financial questions can be answered on the Web

The Web now contains such a vast amount of information it's a virtual library in space. To speed your search through it, you need a librarian. In computerland, librarians are called search engines, such as Excite or Yahoo! These search engines look through the whole Web and bring to your computer screen only what you request—for example, international mutual funds. However, because financial information is so popular, most search engines have created mini-search engines just for personal finance and money. So instead of searching through all of Yahoo! for information on mutual funds, go to **finance.yahoo.com**. (No www. needed.) Here are some of the financial sections within popular search engines you should check out:

Excite—**quicken.excite.com**
Yahoo!—**finance.yahoo.com**
Microsoft—**moneycentral.msn.com**
Netscape—**personalfinance.netscape.com**

To go directly to this site, type in finance.yahoo.com or start at the search engine yahoo.com and follow the channels for financial information.

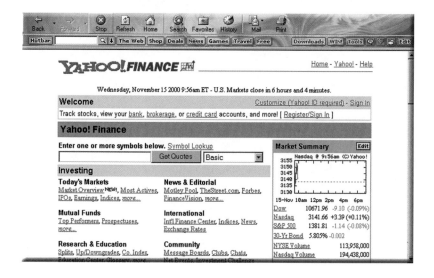

ASK THE EXPERTS

What sites have the latest investment research?

Check out the following sites for information on thousands of stocks, mutual funds, and more:

www.morningstar.com

http://my.zacks.com

What are these calculators that I see on some sites?

Many Web sites include forms that help you determine everything from the size of the mortgage you can afford to the amount of money you need to stash away each year to meet your long-term financial goals. The computer that hosts the Web site calculates the numbers from information you provide and presents an answer tailored to your situation. You can find several useful calculators at **www.financenter.com** or **www.kiplinger.com**.

ALL FINANCE, ALL THE TIME

Sometimes following the market becomes an obsession. When that urge hits, turn to on-line news sources. Some key locations for round-the-clock coverage are:

www.moneycentral.msn.com/investor/
Information as it breaks from one of the leading financial news cable channels.

www.cnnfn.com
Hot stories about business, the economy, and politics.

www.cbs.marketwatch.com
CBS News' site for tracking the day's financial events.

www.thestreet.com
A major source of independent financial news on the Web.

www.fool.com
The Motley Fool provides up-to-date info and down-to-earth advice.

on-line trading

*Making
(or losing)
money on-line*

On-line brokerage firms basically replace the three-piece suit with your computer, or rather your computer's access to the Internet. In essence, you are making security trades directly on-line without anyone's advice. By doing this, on-line brokerage services can lower the fees you pay to buy and sell securities (stocks, bonds, and so on). Many on-line brokerages still have real-life brokers available to assist you over the phone, but you often pay an additional fee for this service.

Numerous on-line brokerages actively trade over the Internet. The following are some popular choices: (Note: you do not need www.)

Excite—**quicken.excite.com**   E-Trade—**etrade.com**

Ameritrade—**ameritrade.com**   Fidelity—**fidelity.com**

Charles Schwab—**schwab.com**   Suretrade—**suretrade.com**

When you set up an on-line account, you can choose from: individual or joint (you or you and your spouse), professional (business), and retirement (IRA) accounts. You will be asked to provide your personal data. Once these are verified, you must sign and return several agreement forms, along with an initial deposit. Then you will be given a user ID and password to log on to your on-line brokerage account. Simply go to your brokerage Web site, type in your password, and start building your portfolio.

On-line brokerage accounts allow you to buy and sell stocks and bonds directly on-line without help from a broker.

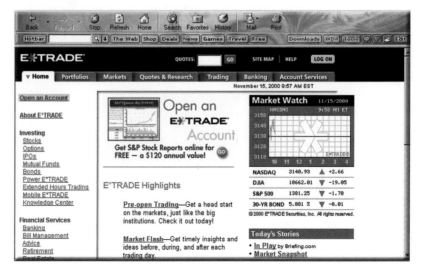

92

ASK THE EXPERTS

What should I look for in an on-line brokerage?

Find out what services they offer either by calling them on the phone or checking out their Web sites. See what kind of research is available and if they charge you to use it. The fee structure for placing orders should be clearly defined.

What are day traders?

Day traders rapidly buy and sell stocks throughout the day in the hope that their stocks will continue climbing or falling in value for the short time—often seconds to minutes—they own the stock, allowing them to lock in quick profits. Day traders usually buy on borrowed money, hoping that they will reap higher profits through leverage, but they also run the risk of higher losses.

FIRST PERSON   DISASTER STORY

On-line Trading Addiction

I feel like I could go on Oprah or something: *The Mom Who Became A Day Trader Junkie*. It started out innocently enough. All I wanted to do was be able to keep a better eye on my stocks so I signed up with an E-trade outfit that gives you instant updates on the stock market. It was so easy to get an E-account, and after one week I made my first trade on-line. I felt very hip. Now all I feel is exhausted. The problem is, it's so easy to check your stocks any time of day or night, that any sudden market move can drive you nuts. Guess what? Sometimes the market shifts every five minutes. There were days when I never left the house. All I did was watch my E-trade account. It got so bad that I missed my daughter's tennis tournament. She came home sobbing because I wasn't there. I knew then that it was time to call it quits. I transferred my whole E-account to a broker. Let him worry about it for me.

Mimi K., Morristown, New Jersey

what's a bond?

What would you do if you needed $50,000 to start your
business? You'd probably take out a loan from a bank, and repay
the bank, with interest. Companies and governments do this, too.
But sometimes they can get a better deal if they go to the markets.
When they need a big chunk of money, they often borrow it from
financial institutions, such as Solomon Smith Barney or Merrill
Lynch. These institutions then split up the loan into a lot of little
loans, beginning at $1,000 or $10,000 each, which they resell to
investors, namely you. Those little loans are called **bonds**. They
work just like a regular loan, in that the company promises to
repay you the money owed (called the **principal**) on a certain date
(the **maturity date**), and in the meantime pays you **interest** on the
loan. Twice a year, the issuer will send you a check containing your
interest earnings. These checks will continue for the life of the
bond.

The nice thing about bonds is that in the end you get your entire
loan back, called the **face** or **par value** of the bond. Say you buy a
bond with a face value of $1,000 that matures in ten years. In ten
years you get your $1,000 back—and don't forget all those twice-
yearly interest checks. Ah, there's the rub. When interest rates rise,
bonds show an ugly side. Suppose you're happily receiving your
check for 6% interest. Suddenly, inflation hits and interest rates
climb to 7%, 8%, and up to 9%. What happens to your check? Not
a thing. You still collect 6%, while it seems that everyone around
you is making more on their investments. You can sell your bond
and get out of this situation, but you'll have to sell it for less than
$1,000 in order to find a buyer.

Here's a little truism about bonds: the market value of a bond
moves in the opposite direction of interest rates. The higher the
interest rate goes, the less valuable your bond is. Why? Because
your bond's interest rate is fixed at a lower rate.

ASK THE EXPERTS

I have a friend who says bonds are great. Then all of a sudden she had to sell some and didn't make a dime. What happened?

You can hold a bond until it matures, but you can sell it ahead of schedule, too. This is where interest rates really affect your bond investment. If your friend had to sell a 6% bond when market rates on similar bonds were at 7% or 8%, no investor in his right mind would buy her bond for what she paid for it. Why? Because that investor could buy a new one that pays higher interest. So your friend would have to sell it at a **discount**, or a price below face value. But say interest rates fall below 6%. Then her bond would look a lot more attractive. She could sell it for more than she paid (called a **premium**) because investors want her bond's higher interest payments.

The bonds I invested in are being called in. What does that mean?

When bonds are **called** it means the borrower is buying back the bonds sooner than it had agreed to as stated on the bond's maturity date. Typically, this happens when interest rates drop and the borrower wants to "retire" its high **interest rate** bonds so it can issue bonds at a less expensive interest rate. And no, there is nothing you can do about it, except start looking around for other bonds to invest in. (Most bonds have an initial length of time when they cannot be called, usually 5 to 10 years after they have been issued.)

I heard that some bonds are tax free?

To encourage investing in public projects, such as schools and airports, the feds made the interest earned on most **municipal bonds** tax free on your federal tax return. (That said, you usually have to pay state income tax on the interest you earn.) Because of this federal tax-free benefit, municipal bonds usually pay less interest than corporate bonds.

types of bonds

Fixed interest payments

If stocks are the high-end items on a menu, then bonds are the blue plate specials. Day in and day out it's the same deal: interest income. The only thing that affects them is interest rates. That said, there are all sorts of bonds to choose from. They are categorized according to who issues them and their maturity dates.

The only way the U.S. government can raise money is by issuing bonds. (Okay, well, there are taxes, and that neat thing they do at the Mint, known as printing money.) The U.S. Treasury Department is the official bond issuer for the feds. As with all bonds, how much interest the issuer pays is wrapped up in the bond's time frame. Short-term bonds are called "T-bills" in bondland and they have a low yield; medium-term bonds are called "T-notes" and have a moderate yield; long-term bonds are called "T-bonds" and they have one of the highest yields around but the government no longer issues these. (You owe federal taxes on interest you earn, but you don't have to pay state taxes on it.)

When states and local governments issue bonds they are called municipal bonds. They can be short- or long-term and pay various interest rates. Generally they are considered safe investments. One big advantage to them is that the interest you earn is usually exempt from federal taxes.

Corporate bonds fall into two main categories: quality and junk. Yep, they really are called junk. Quality bonds are issued by companies that are considered financially stable. Junk bonds are issued by companies whose stability is questionable, which is why they offer a higher interest rate. Junk bonds are a classic example of taking more risk to get more profit.

ASK THE EXPERTS

What's a zero-coupon bond?

Any bond you buy earns interest—even if you don't get it right away, which is the case with zero-coupon bonds. Here you buy a bond, be it issued by the government or a corporation, at a deeply discounted price. As you hold the bond, its price increases until it reaches its maturity date, when you get back its full face value. You get no actual interest payments, but you have to pay taxes on what you would have gotten. Yes, it's tricky; you need to ask your tax advisor about this, not your broker, if you're thinking about buying one. Why buy one? It helps ensure that you have money far off in the future for big-ticket items such as college tuition (see page 58) or retirement (see page 154).

A BREAKDOWN ON BONDS

Issuer	Maturity	Type	Yield	Safety*
U.S. Government	short	T-bills	low	best
U.S. Government	medium	T-notes	medium	best
U.S. Agencies	medium	mortgages	high	better
Municipal (general)	all	G.O.**	varies	better
Municipal (revenue)	all	revenue	varies	good
Money market	short	varies	low	better
Blue chip corporate	all	bonds	medium	good
Junk bond corporate	all	junk bonds	high	poor

*Safety is defined as the opposite of default, where the issue declines to pay interest or even principal.
**General obligation

what's a mutual fund?

The best place for newbie investors

If stocks are the à la carte items on a menu and bonds the blue plate specials, then mutual funds are the equivalent of a buffet. They offer an easy way to sample dozens, hundreds, even thousands of stocks, bonds, and other financial instruments without having to invest in each one individually. Who chooses what goes into this financial smorgasbord? **The portfolio fund manager** and a team of financial experts who spend their days looking for top investments to increase the value of their fund. They then sell shares of their fund to investors, i.e., you. The more people who invest, the more investments it can buy and the bigger its total assets become. The greater the assets, the more clout it has in the market. Best of all, with so many riches in the trove, if one stock flops or a company calls in a bond, hundreds of others cushion the blow. Talk about diversification!

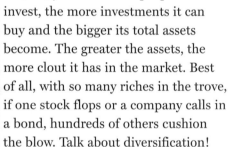

What should you look for in a mutual fund? Long-term performance, meaning a steady return over the years. To assess that performance, take a look at the fund's scorecard, its **prospectus**, a pamphlet that you can ask the fund to send you. It lists the fund's objectives, holdings, performance, and fees. You don't have to slog through the whole thing—most of the juicy stuff is on the first few pages. Look for a solid **total return**. Total return is the amount the fund earned (dividends plus capital gains distributions plus increase in share price), minus expenses and fees. Those 5- and 10-year total return charts are the ultimate performance measure. Just make sure that the current portfolio manager was on board during the time period that you're reviewing.

ASK THE EXPERTS

How do I keep track of my mutual fund's price?

Look for something called the fund's **Net Asset Value** or **NAV**. It's nothing more than the value of all the stocks and bonds the fund owns, divided by the number of the fund's shares owned by its investors. In other words, if the fund had $2 billion worth of stocks, bonds, etc., and investors owned 100 million shares of the fund, then the fund's NAV would be $20. That's how much a share in the fund would cost. Because the prices of stocks and bonds change every day, so does a fund's NAV. That's why it's listed daily in the financial section of most newspapers.

Do funds charge fees or commissions to buy into them?

Some funds charge a commission to buy shares in their funds. Others don't. Those that charge commissions are called **load funds**. You can buy them from a stockbroker, an investment advisor, or directly from the fund company. Some load funds tack on a **redemption** fee if you sell your shares prematurely. (Typically, funds like you to hang in there for at least seven years. If you sell before that, they can zap you with a redemption fee.) Others have a **back-end load**, meaning you pay a fee when you sell. Quite a few are **no-load funds**, meaning you buy shares in the fund directly from the fund and you don't have to pay any middlemen commissions. However, there may be other fees involved to cover distribution, marketing, and sales of the fund each year. Read a **prospectus** carefully.

I'd like to invest in mutual funds, but I don't have enough money to meet the minimum. What can I do?

Lots of funds require a minimum investment, but many will waive the minimum if you open an IRA account (see page 156), or if you agree to automatically deposit at least $50 a month directly from your bank account. This is a great way to build up your investment without worrying about whether or not you're buying in at the right time. Buying monthly also ensures that you buy more shares when the fund is cheap, and fewer when shares are more expensive. This is called **dollar cost averaging** and is an excellent way to invest. If you go this route, just be sure to hang on to your monthly statements, since the tax consequences of selling these shares later can get tricky.

choosing a fund

Find the fund that fits you best

What funds should you invest in? Buy shares in funds that match your financial objectives, be they short-, medium- or long-term. (See page 66.) For example, if you're saving for your toddler's college, target growth or aggressive growth funds. If you're retired and you need an investment whose return you can live on, explore income or growth and income funds, which will generate income each month. Or if you're a beginning investor with a long time frame, but you haven't quite figured out your goals and risk tolerance, start with either a balanced fund, which contains relatively predictable stocks and bonds, or an S&P index fund to build a solid stock foundation.

Remember: commissions, administrative fees, and other operating costs can shrink returns like a wool sweater in the dryer. Check out how much the fund spends to run itself: these are its **operating expenses**. Compare that to a fund's total assets. This is called its **expense ratio**. Anything over 2% is too pricey.

MUTUAL FUND CATEGORIES

Because there are over 10,000 mutual funds available, it's important to decide what type to buy before you start shopping.

STOCK FUNDS: tend to be categorized by the size of companies they invest in, how fast these companies grow, and their location.

Size: Small companies ("small-cap" companies), medium-size companies ("mid-caps"), and large companies ("large-caps") often react differently to market news. While small-caps tend to be riskier, over time they may provide higher returns. It's good to have a mix of all three.

Style: Growth funds invest in companies whose earnings are growing very quickly. Value funds hold stocks that managers dig up in the bargain basement—these stocks either fell from grace, or seem inexpensive compared to how much they are making. When the prices of these stocks start climbing, managers unload them and reap the profits.

Geographic: Most stock funds are domestic, meaning they are invested in companies inside the United States. *International funds* invest in companies outside the U.S., while *emerging market funds*, considered a riskier investment, focus on companies outside the U.S. such as Latin America and Eastern Europe. *Global funds* invest in both international and domestic companies. (While most international funds buy stocks, they also purchase international bonds.)

BOND FUNDS: (also called **Fixed-Income Funds**) are classified by the types of bonds they invest in or the bond's average maturity (see page 97). These funds generate a stream of income for investors, and their prices tend to fluctuate less than stock funds.

CASH FUNDS: (also called **Money Market Mutual Funds**) consist of bonds with extremely short-term maturity dates (30 to 90 days). They are virtually risk free.

CHECK IT OUT

Before you buy a fund, check out how it's doing by comparing it to similar funds. A financial company called Morningstar rates the performance of nearly all funds on the market. Five stars means the fund is tops in its category; one star means it's the lowest. Morningstar also analyzes the history of the fund and its managers.

MUTUAL FUND OBJECTIVES

So now you know a bit about what the manager likes to invest in. But what are his or her objectives? There are basically four to choose from:

Aggressive growth—These risky funds usually invest in high-tech stocks that tend to have higher than expected returns, but might lose money, too.

Growth—This type of fund is looking for less risky growth, and holds more stable blue chip stocks.

Growth and Income—These funds may invest in stocks with high-paying dividends, or might combine stocks and bonds to provide income along with growth.

Income—These funds hold safe, income-producing assets, usually bonds, with a few dividend-paying stocks tossed in.

your portfolio

*Putting it
all together*

When you build a house, you need to lay out how big each room will be. Same goes for your financial portfolio—you need to figure out your **asset allocation**, a fancy term for planning how much you want to invest in which investment vehicles: stocks and stock funds, bonds and bond funds, and cash, such as money market accounts.

Your age figures prominently in the mix when you construct your portfolio. The younger you are, the more you can turn to stocks, as you have lots of time to recover in case things falter. As you age and your expenses mount, you may not be able to afford such daring, so you reallocate funds to more bonds and fewer stocks. Then, when your goals are imminent and you need to protect your principal, you invest even less money in stocks.

How to figure out the asset mix that is right for you? For a very broad guideline, subtract your age from 110. The difference represents the percentage of your portfolio that you put into stocks or stock mutual funds. The rest goes to income or cash. Suppose you're 45. Subtract 45 from 110 and you get 65, so at least 65% of your portfolio should be in stocks. This leaves 35% for bonds and cash (equally, bond funds or money-markets).

Once you sketch your broad guidelines, fill in the details by figuring out how to invest within those guidelines. In other words, think about the kinds of rooms you need first, then about how to furnish them. For example, once you opt for 65% stocks, you can further divide that: one-fourth into high-tech stocks, one fourth into international stocks, and one-half into blue chip stocks, depending on your risk tolerance and return needs. Check out the chart on page 73 to figure out your risk tolerance.

SK THE EXPERTS

When should I change from one type of investment into another?

Watch your time, as you need to adjust your portfolio as each goal approaches. If you need a certain amount of money in less than five years, to pay for college, for example, make sure the money isn't in stocks. As the goal approaches, slowly move the money into more conservative investments such as a CD, money market, or Treasury bill.

How should I factor my retirement investments into my asset allocation?

Use your 401(k) or retirement plan as your foundation. This is the best place for high-earning investments that would otherwise generate lots of taxes because the taxes are deferred until you reach retirement age. (After retirement, since you won't be working, your tax bracket should drop; the lower your tax bracket, the less taxes you will have to pay on money you are making now.)

YOUR ANNUAL FISCAL PHYSICAL

Every year give your portfolio a physical to make sure it's still on track to meet your goals and that all parts are healthy. Check mutual funds against similar types of funds. Refer to the Morningstar reports (see page 101). If you're not on course, you may have to change things a bit, such as switch mutual funds, or hold the funds and postpone a financial goal. If you need to do some adjusting because you have too much of one type of asset and not enough of another, you don't need to get rid of anything. Instead, put new savings into the vehicle you need to load up on.

now what do I do?
Answers to common questions

My son starts college in two years, and my sister says we should put his tuition money into Treasuries. What are these?

Treasuries, the safest bonds of all, are sold and backed by the U.S. government. **Treasury bills,** also called T-bills, mature in 13, 26, or 52 weeks and are a great place to park money that's destined for an imminent goal. You don't receive interest payments on these bonds; they're sold at a discount. **Treasury notes** (or T-notes) are another option. These mature in two to 10 years and yield a bit more than T-bills. T-notes are ideal for retirees and people with medium-term goals who can't afford to endanger their principal.

I'm in a high tax bracket, and I heard that municipal bonds could be good for me. But the interest rates don't seem very appealing.

Municipal bonds (also known as munis) are issued by state or local governments. True, they yield a bit less than Treasuries, but don't let that fool you. The interest munis pay is exempt from federal taxes. And, in many states, if you buy munis issued in the state in which you live, they're exempt from state taxes, too! Municipal bonds cost upwards of $5,000 apiece, but even without buying one, you can still reap their benefits by investing in mutual funds that carry munis.

How do I diversify if I just want to buy mutual funds?

One good way is to evenly divide the money you want to invest in mutual funds into three or four different types of funds. For example, put a quarter in a growth fund; a quarter in a value fund; a quarter in a bond fund; and a quarter in an international fund. This way you spread the risk around. If you don't have enough money to buy into several different funds, consider a "fund of funds" or a "lifestyle fund" that invests in several different mutual funds, thereby doing the diversifying for you.

How long does it take to buy or sell a stock?

It depends. If you don't set a price limit on the transaction, it's however much time your broker needs to pick up the phone and call his firm's trading desk. That said, if you want to buy or sell at a specific price, or if there's a big imbalance between the number of people who want to sell and those wanting to buy, it may take hours or even a full day to sell your shares of stock.

What about investing in real estate?

Ah, real estate. Like stocks, real estate has growth potential, if the buildings' values go up; and like bonds, real estate can produce income from the rent that's collected. Sound like the perfect investment? Don't forget about risk—many real estate investments are as risky, if not riskier, than investing in stock. If you want to throw a few dimes into real estate, consider investing in a Real Estate Investment Trust (REIT). A REIT is a publicly traded fund that owns a group of buildings (offices, apartment buildings, strip malls). Better yet, for more diversification, consider one of the many mutual funds that invest in real estate by purchasing many different REITs. Finally, don't forget about your home! Don't think that it's not an investment, just because you live there.

My company's stock just split. What does that mean?

Companies often declare a stock split if the price of their stock becomes too high, say, over $100. Why? Shareholders generally buy stock in bundles of 100, and if a stock price becomes too high, it gets difficult for average investors to afford to buy the stock. For example, if you owned 100 shares of a company that split, you now own 200 shares. And if it was trading at $150 before the split, it's probably trading closer to $75 per share now.

Helpful Resources

WEB SITES	BOOKS
www.morningstar.com The first place to go when researching mutual funds.	**Investing for Dummies** by Eric Tyson
www.quicken.com A great collection of personal finance information and tools. Helps you research stocks and create a strategy for building a sound portfolio.	**The Only Investment Guide You'll Ever Need** by Andrew Tobias
www.smartmoney.com Helpful investment information from *SmartMoney* magazine.	**The Everything Money Book** by Rich Mintzer and Kathi Mintzer
www.aaii.com Site of the American Association of Individual Investors. Has information on stocks, bonds, and portfolio management.	**The Late-Start Investor** by John F. Wasik

Insurance

6

INSURANCE

66 While insurance can never fix the emotional damage a loss wreaks, it can protect you against financial loss. 99

covering your assets

Protect yourself and your stuff from all unforeseen losses

There is no way around it; you're always at risk of losing what you have. That's why there's insurance—to protect you and your loved ones from financial consequences if disaster strikes.

Insurance works like this: you figure out how much money you need to replace the lost or damaged item. For example, if it would cost you $100,000 to rebuild your home if it were destroyed, then that's how much insurance you would need. An insurance company will sell you a policy stating that they will pay for, or "cover," certain damages up to a total replacement of $100,000. The company will then determine the premium, or how much it will charge you each year for this coverage.

While insurance can never fix the emotional damage a loss wreaks, it can protect you against financial loss. The best rule of thumb about insurance is to buy enough to protect you, if replacing the loss with your own money would be prohibitively expensive.

ASK THE EXPERTS

What is a policy?

It's a contract that the insurance company writes, detailing the amount they pay you if disaster strikes. It also lists which kinds of disasters are covered and which are not.

Is there a cost relationship between your deductible and your premium?

Yes. The lower your deductible (the amount you agree to pay before your insurance company starts paying), the higher your premium (your monthly, quarterly, or annual insurance payment).

What is the difference between "actual cash value" and "replacement value" coverage?

It's the difference between old and new. If your five-year-old TV is stolen, your insurance company only pays what a five-year-old TV is worth today, assuming you opted for "actual cash value." If you have "replacement value" coverage, then it pays what it costs to replace it. Read the replacement cost part of your insurance policy carefully, and ask your insurance agent or financial advisor exactly how it will affect your home and other belongings. If you want full replacement coverage, it will cost more than regular coverage.

life insurance

Once you've come to terms with the inevitable, you'll want to name your beneficiaries

Life insurance is really income insurance, meaning that in the event of your death your life insurance is supposed to make up for the money you would have earned in the future. An insurance company usually pays this amount in a lump sum, called a **death benefit**. You need life insurance if anyone will suffer financially if you die. If you have young children or college-bound kids, for example, insurance on your life is critical.

How much insurance do you need? It all depends on what your dependents would need financially to soldier on after your death. If you have little children and a non-working spouse, you need a lot. Experts suggest that when children are involved, you should leave six times your annual income. If you have no dependents, and your spouse is gainfully employed, you only need enough to cover your debts, your funeral expenses, and perhaps a year or so of your income.

If you do need life insurance, the next question is, which type is best for you? There are two main options: term or permanent. **Term insurance** provides coverage for a fixed length of time, such as 5, 10, or 20 years. You pay a monthly, quarterly or annual **premium** or fee for the term you wish to insure. If you die before your term limit, your loved ones get a death benefit; if you live past it, your insurance expires and there is no coverage. On the other hand, **permanent insurance** doesn't expire; it also has a savings feature known as a cash value that you can borrow against or use to supplement your savings.

Where can you find out about insurance companies and the types of insurance policies they sell? Look for insurance firms that are rated at AA or better; check them out at www.ambest.com. Look closely at the company, not just the agent.

ASK THE EXPERTS

How much life insurance do I need?

First, figure out how much money your family needs each year for bills, debt, and expenses such as child care, home maintenance, and tuition. Subtract any other money your dependents might receive (a spouse's salary, perhaps). Then determine how long it will be before your children finish school or college and your spouse starts receiving retirement benefits. Now multiply the annual amount by the number of years. This gives you a ballpark figure for your death benefit. Many insurers suggest that you buy a death benefit that is at least six times your annual income, but the ideal amount really depends on the ages of your children, your income, and your family's spending habits.

Where can I find inexpensive insurance coverage?

Many companies, trade groups, and other associations offer life insurance at reasonable prices. Insurance agents can give you suggestions, but bear in mind that they may recommend one company over another only because it pays them higher commissions, and not because it is the best buy for you. Some companies sell policies directly to an individual; they are called "low-load" or "no-load" policies since they carry either low or no commissions.

How much will life insurance cost?

Costs depend first on the size of the death benefit. Your age, sex, health, and the type of policy (term or permanent), all affect the premium. Here are factors that can raise the premium:

- You are over 50 years of age
- You smoke
- You are obese
- You have a bad driving record
- You take certain medicines

Don't try to fudge these factors on your application. The insurance company thoroughly investigates before it sells you a policy.

INSURANCE AGENTS

There are two types of insurance agents: One who works for just one company, is called a captive or exclusive agent. The other, called an independent agent, represents several different companies.

Most agents generally recommend permanent life insurance policies over term life insurance because they get higher commissions selling permanent life than for selling term. The sales pitches also don't tell you that your premiums include administrative and investment management fees. If you're buying a permanent policy make sure it's for a good reason, for example, to lock yourself into a savings schedule.

term life insurance

With term insurance, you pay only for the basics

RED●FLAG

If you truly haven't saved a dime, and you have youngsters but no insurance, drop this book now and immediately pick up some term life insurance.

Term life insurance is simple: If you die during the term of your policy, your beneficiary gets a death benefit. Period. That's it. If you outlive your term insurance, then your beneficiary doesn't get a dime and you don't get back any of the premiums you've paid (as you would if you had permanent life insurance).

Term insurance is fairly inexpensive because you pay only for insurance. To buy $300,000 in coverage, a healthy 30-year-old man might pay about $375 a year compared to five times that amount for permanent insurance. But costs for term insurance can swing wildly from one company to the next. When shopping, compare premium costs, benefits paid, and how many years the term covers. Also ask about the following features, all of which can affect the cost:

Guaranteed renewability: The insurance company must renew your policy at the end of the term, even if you're in ill health.

Annual renewable term: The policy automatically renews each year, but as you age, the premiums increase. At first it's cheaper than level term (see below), but it gets more costly as time passes. Calculate the premiums to see which is better over the length of time you need.

Guaranteed level premium: You pay a fixed premium for a certain number of years. Common terms are 5, 10, or 20 years.

Decreasing term: Your premium is fixed, but your death benefit decreases each year.

Guaranteed convertible: You can convert a term policy into a permanent policy with the same amount of coverage, without a physical exam or further scrutiny of your insurability.

Disability waiver rider: If you become disabled, you no longer have to pay your premiums to keep the policy going.

Accelerated death benefit rider: If you become terminally ill, and have two years or less to live, you may be able to receive death benefits before you die.

permanent life insurance

Permanent insurance provides redeemable cash value as well as protection

The biggest selling point for permanent life insurance is that in addition to paying a **death benefit** (a lump sum paid when you die), it lets you build up tax-deferred savings that you can keep if you decide to terminate the policy. In other words, you get back some of the money you've been paying in premiums. Many people use this money to supplement their retirement income.

There are several types:

Whole life: This type of policy guarantees a lump sum to your beneficiary. It also builds up a cash value, which you receive if you surrender the policy before you die. The premiums you pay do not change, and the amount of the benefit your beneficiary would receive in the event of your death remains fixed. The cash value you could withdraw grows at a fixed rate of return as long as you pay your premiums.

Universal life: This is whole life with a twist. The guaranteed minimum annual return is higher than what you might earn with a whole life policy, but that return varies each year, based largely on the life insurance company's investments. You can choose to increase or decrease the premium as well as the death benefit.

Variable life: Your premium stays fixed, and you get to choose how part of it gets invested (the company controls investment of the other part). The success of these investments determines how much your beneficiary ends up with, in addition to a guaranteed minimum lump sum at your death.

Variable universal life: It's a combination of variable and universal life in that it offers flexible premiums and investment options.

disability insurance

Your most valuable asset—your present earning power—must be protected, too

Life insurance gives you a certain peace of mind—that your loved ones will be taken care of financially when you're gone. But what if you break your leg tomorrow and you're unable to work for a while? Who will pay your bills? Not only will you have limited, if any, income, but your broken leg will most likely generate even more bills for chores you can no longer do yourself.

That's where disability income insurance comes in. If you are unable to work, disability (as it's called in insuranceland) kicks in and pays you a percentage of your lost salary every month. For this income safety net, you pay the insurance company a premium. Many people ignore disability insurance; but the fact is, for most folks there's a greater chance of being injured and unable to work than of actually dying. Grim as that sounds, buying disability insurance beats thinking about what to do if you end up not only flat on your back, but also worrying about how to make ends meet.

The smaller your savings nest egg, the more you need disability income insurance. In essence, it insures your earning power—a much greater asset than your home or your car, yet one that tends to be overlooked when it comes to insurance protection. The benefits don't total 100% of your salary (otherwise, there wouldn't be much incentive to get back to work, would there?), but they can cover 60%, depending on the policy. Coverage comes with a hefty price tag, however, since there's usually a higher chance you'll use disability income insurance than, say, term life insurance.

When you shop for disability insurance, look for these guarantees: fixed monthly payment; a policy that stays in effect as long as you pay your premium, even if you're sick; and the opportunity to buy more benefits without having to prove your continued good health (a must if you expect your income or your financial obligations to rise).

ASK THE EXPERTS

My brother injured his leg but couldn't collect disability payments because the insurance company said he could still work for his employer, even though it would mean taking a different job. Is this right?

That depends on how his policy defines "disabled." Disability policies grant vastly different coverage. Many policies only pay up if you can't find any type of job in your industry. If you're a dentist, for example, and you lose your fingers in a car-door accident, that disability would prevent you from tending to teeth, but not from teaching dentistry, so you might not get benefits. But a policy that offers *own occupation* coverage would pay because you are unable to perform the duties your current occupation requires. (Social Security Disability Insurance (SSDI) kicks in if you're severely disabled.)

Disability insurance is so expensive. What factors affect my premiums?

1. How long you will get benefits. A policy that pays throughout your lifetime costs more than one that pays up to a certain age.

2. How much you get paid. The higher the benefits, the steeper the premium.

3. The waiting period, or how long you'll wait from the time you become disabled until your benefits begin. Wait at least three to six months and you'll slash premium costs.

4. Also, consider these features and riders: automatic increase in benefits or cost-of-living adjustments to cover inflation; residual benefits, paying a partial benefit if your disability prevents you from working full-time, but you can work part-time; a waiver of premiums preventing them from rising if you become disabled. They are pricey, but get them if you can afford them.

home insurance

Defend your domicile from disaster

Your home is supposed to keep you safe and sound, but what happens if misfortune knocks at the door? Fire, theft, flood, you name it, it all spells the same thing: financial loss. That's why there is homeowner's insurance; it covers losses and damage to the structure of your home and to your personal property. (If you are a renter, check into renter's insurance to cover any losses.) If you are carrying a mortgage on your home, you probably already have an existing homeowner's policy. But it may not be enough to cover your actual losses.

To determine how much coverage you need, first figure out how much it would cost to rebuild your home if it were damaged or destroyed. Ask a builder for an estimate based on materials and labor costs in your neighborhood, your home's square footage, and features such as central air-conditioning, stone hearth, parquet floors, custom windows, and other special features you have.

Next, figure out how much it would cost to replace your possessions inside the house. (Renters, you need to do this.) Go from room to room and estimate how much the items in it would cost today, then add it all up for a ballpark figure. (You'll learn how to do a home inventory on page 118.)

Now add the value of your home's contents to the cost of rebuilding the structure. You need to buy a replacement cost policy for the total amount of rebuilding your house and replacing everything in it. Without it, you might be unpleasantly surprised if you ever have to make a claim. For example, a policy that stipulates payment for actual cash value pays only what the damaged or missing contents are worth after **depreciation** (loss of value over time). So if a thief absconds with your 12-year-old TV, a 6-year-old CD player, your leather jacket from college, and a 4-year-old fax machine, the check from the insurance company will not come close to buying these items today.

ASK THE EXPERTS

What can I do to reduce my homeowner's insurance rates?

Buy smoke detectors, fire extinguishers, deadbolt locks, and a security system (if it's hooked up to a central monitoring system, you save even more). And get cracking on those home improvements. A new roof, upgraded wiring, and new pipes will lower your rates, too. Raise your **deductible** (the amount of damages you agree to pay before the insurance company starts paying) as much as you can afford. Sometimes hiking it from $250 to $500 can cut your premium by 10%. And here's one more reason to quit smoking: you pay less to insure a smoke-free home than one with a smoker.

My homeowner's insurance doesn't cover all my jewelry. What should I do?

You need a **rider** (a separate policy) that covers particular items you want to insure, such as jewelry, electronics, furs, silver, guns, boats, or your Pez-dispenser collection. Before you buy a rider, though, estimate what the items would cost to replace. If the loss won't set you back much, say, for a ratty old raccoon coat and your granny's small diamond brooch, it isn't worth paying the extra premium for the rider.

What is liability insurance and how much do I need?

Liability insurance protects you from the cost of litigation if someone is injured in your home. For example, if your dog bites the neighbor, a party guest slips on a wayward nacho, or your babysitter trips over your toddler's toys. Most homeowner policies provide at least $100,000 of liability coverage. Because the chances are slim that these things will happen to you, getting additional liability coverage is not too expensive, usually $25 a month for a million dollars or so in coverage. To get more coverage, take out an **umbrella** liability policy; it extends the liability protection that comes with your homeowner's coverage and your car insurance policy. You should have enough liability insurance to cover your **net worth** (see page 171).

taking a home inventory

Keep track of what you own

It's smart to create a home inventory before any disaster occurs, in case you need proof for future claims. This is a time consuming task. But it's absolutely vital if you want to safeguard what you've accumulated. Set aside an hour or two each weekend until you've covered your whole house. First, make a list of the most expensive things in each room. Simply walk around with a notebook and start writing. Don't forget to note what's inside the bureau drawers, the closets, and the cabinets, as well as the basement, attic, and garage. If you can, write down when you bought each item and how much you paid for it. If you're not sure, estimate, as you have to come up with a value in order to get insurance. Note brands, designers or model numbers, and include any receipts you have, or appraisals (include the name and address of the appraiser).

Supplement your list using a video or digital camera, so you have a visual record. Review the inventory once a year to make sure it's up to date. (If you prefer, you can log the contents of your entire house with home-inventory software.) Don't keep your inventory notebook, videotape, or photographs in the house; store them in a safe deposit box in the bank for safe keeping.

118

INSURANCE AGENTS

While buying through an agent is the most expensive route, insurance agents who work exclusively for one insurance company generally provide helpful information and advice. Independent agents who represent various companies also provide helpful info and advice, and may have a wider array of products to suit your needs. Ask for referrals from your lawyer, financial planner, accountant, or friends. Rule out anyone who tries to pressure you into a policy or sell you an insurance product you don't need. Select an agent who acts more like an advisor looking after your needs than a salesperson.

FIRST PERSON   **SUCCESS STORY**

Videotape to the Rescue

Last year we had a fire in our house. It started so quickly, we hardly had time to call 911. But thank heavens, the fire fighters were able to put it out and just the kitchen, dining room, and entranceway were damaged. When the shock began to wear off, we realized with a start that we hadn't updated our home inventory list in fifteen years. Then we remembered that last year we had had our 25th wedding anniversary party professionally videotaped. We were able to use the videotape to establish many of the things we had neglected to add to our out-of-date list. It really helped when it came time to settle with the insurance company.

Sarah T., Kansas City, Kansas

auto insurance

Steer clear of road-related hazards

If you have a car, you're already familiar with automobile insurance, since in the United States you can't register a car without it. The premise is simple: you pay the premiums and (depending on your coverage) the insurance company will pay to fix or replace your damaged car, as well as expenses related to any injury, rehabilitative care, and lost earnings of anyone hurt by your car. Without this insurance, an accident could put the brakes on your savings, as you would be liable for sizable damages that could be a burden for the rest of your life.

Not surprisingly, the **liability coverage** for bodily injury claims and property damage claims determines most of the cost of auto insurance. The more you can afford, the more you should get. You also need to include the following in your insurance:

Uninsured- or underinsured-motorist coverage: It compensates you and your passengers if a negligent driver doesn't have enough insurance to pay your bills.

Medical or PIP insurance: This covers medical bills and lost wages for you and any passengers injured in your car.

Collision insurance: This pays for repair or replacement parts for your car if damaged in a crash.

Comprehensive insurance: This covers damage from other sources, such as theft, vandalism, broken glass, fire, falling objects, and storms.

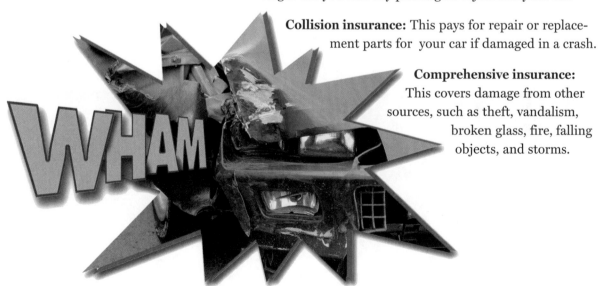

WHAT HELPS TO DETERMINE THE COST OF YOUR POLICY?

In addition to the different types of coverage listed on the opposite page, you might want to consider the following options to lower your premium:

Your deductible: To save money on your premium, raise the deductible, and pay for small damages and losses from your emergency fund.

Where you live and how far you drive: For example, a person who lives in New York and commutes 30 miles to work pays a higher premium than a person who lives in Iowa and commutes five miles to work.

The type of car you drive: To save on premiums, choose a car that costs less to repair. Also avoid cars that are favorites among thieves. For a list of cars thieves love but insurers hate, check out the Insurance News Network listing at www.insure.com.

Your driving record: Contest tickets and moving violations, which raise your rates. Take any state-approved defensive-driving or drug and alcohol awareness class that will lower your rates.

Your age: Younger drivers tend to have more accidents, so their insurance comes at a higher price—thousands of dollars a year for young males. To save money, encourage Junior to keep his grades up. This evidence of conscientiousness may persuade your insurance company to give you a slightly better rate.

Your smoking habits: If you light up, your car insurance premium goes up.

Your car's safety and anti-theft features: Request a discount if your car has automatic seat belts or air bags, anti-lock brakes, wheel locks, an ignition cut-off system, or an alarm system.

If your car isn't worth much more than $1,000, skip the collision coverage and pocket the premium payment. That amount, plus the deductible, would equal what you'd get if the car were totaled.

making a claim

If disaster strikes, you'll need lists of everything you own—including the kitchen sink—to get what you're due

When you make a claim, how much do you get? To assess your loss and decide on the amount to be reimbursed, the insurance company sends a company adjuster (or an approved repairman) to look at your car or house. You tell the adjuster what was damaged and the adjuster offers you a settlement—a cash payment to cover most of the damage. Sounds simple, but it may not be. What if you and the adjuster disagree over what was lost? Then you need to prove your claims. No matter what the amount, your best tactic for getting what you want is having good records.

Good records aren't something you can prepare when disaster strikes. Suppose the damage is to your house. You need to have records showing that the damaged item, for example the roof, was in good condition before the disaster struck. Have maintenance and repair records ready when you talk with an adjuster. See page 118 to guide you through taking a home inventory.

Don't keep your inventory notebook, videotape, or photographs in the house; store them in a safe deposit box in the bank for safe keeping.

IT'S AN OFFER YOU CAN REFUSE

If you're not satisfied with the amount the insurance company offers you to fix or replace your house or car, you don't have to accept it. Do your own figuring and renegotiate. First hire your own appraiser to estimate the damage. (Your state insurance agency may have a list of licensed appraisers.) Then start haggling—with the insurance company's adjusters, supervisors, and managers. Get your insurance agent to weigh in and support your claim. Perhaps a person from your company's benefits office also will help. You might even try contacting a representative from your state's department of insurance.

Keep a record of the dates and times you talk to your insurer, and get the representatives' names. Take notes during the conversations. Log all bills resulting from the claims process, including medical, baby-sitting, home health care, housekeeping, car rental, takeout food—whatever expenses result from the loss—and add them to your claim.

Remember, persistence is your best ally in pursuing a better settlement.

Be aware that a repair shop on your insurer's approved list may compromise quality to keep the insurer's costs down. Before you authorize any repairs, insist on OEM (original equipment manufacturer) parts, and refuse LKQ (like kind and quality) parts, which may not fit as well, nor match in color.

health insurance

The trick is finding the right plan for your situation

There are basically two possibilities when it comes to health insurance. Either your employer offers health insurance or you need to find your own. Most corporations pay for at least part of their employees' health insurance. (Some even offer several types of plans to choose from.) But as the costs of health care continue to rise, the cost of health insurance is rising, too. Some companies may ask you to pay a larger share. You will, however, continue to enjoy the advantage of their group rates, which are generally less expensive than rates for individuals. (Most health insurance does not include long-term care. For more on that, see page 159.)

If you need to find your own health insurance, try contacting Quotesmith at www.quotesmith.com, which has a list of health-care plans with descriptions of coverage and premium costs. Look for the most recent evaluation of health plans in Consumer Reports. Your state's insurance agency also can provide price surveys, as well as reports on the number of complaints they receive about insurers.

When changing jobs or buying your own insurance, ask about coverage for pre-existing health conditions—health problems that you've had for a while, such as asthma or diabetes. Some insurers wait up to a year before they start paying the bills for them; a few won't cover them at all. Also, look for unlimited lifetime care on your policy, or a maximum limit no lower than $1 million. After all, you'll want the best of care if you're ever faced with a heart attack, cancer, or some crippling disease or accident.

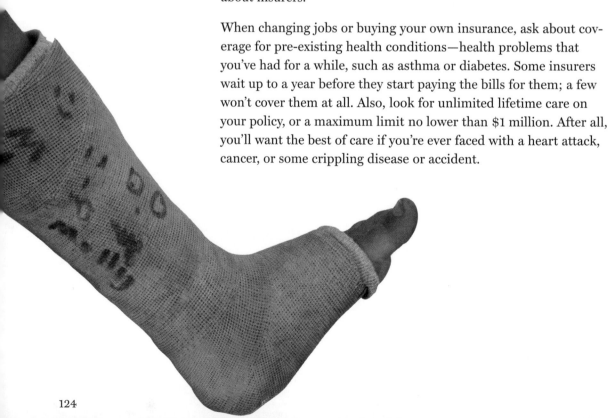

ASK THE EXPERTS

What is an HMO, and how does it work?

A health maintenance organization, or HMO, is the type of health insurance plan that assigns your care to a doctor within its doctors' group (often housed together in a clinic-type office). Any other health care is subject to that doctor's approval and is performed only by specialists and hospitals within, or designated by, the HMO. The fees you pay for medical services are nominal. But if you see physicians or seek hospital care outside the HMO, you'll pay the costs in full.

How does a preferred-provider or point-of-service health insurance plan work?

These types of health care insurance plans allow you to choose your primary care physician from a list of participants who have agreed to accept a set schedule of fees proposed by the insurance company. Once you choose a primary care physician, some plans require your primary care doctor to approve any other health care you receive. You pay more for this kind of insurance than for an HMO, and the co-payments (fees you pay for medical services) are likely to be higher as well. Sometimes these insurers provide options for seeing doctors or going to hospitals that are not listed in their plan—if you pay a greater percentage of the costs. The service you receive, however, is often better than with an HMO.

now what do I do?

Answers to common questions

Assuming that I know exactly what a policy will cover, should I get a list of quotes and buy the lowest-priced policy?

Not necessarily. Whether you buy insurance from your uncle or from a AAA rated firm, coverage is only as good as the insurance company's ability to pay you. Before you buy, check out the insurance company's financial strength, credibility, and payment history. A.M. Best rates all major insurance firms (see www.ambest.com). You can get a list of the least reputable companies at www.weissratings.com.

My employer doesn't offer health insurance, and the individual insurance plans are really expensive. Is there any way to get a more reasonable rate?

Check with professional or alumni associations or trade groups you belong to; many offer group plans to their members that are cheaper than individual health insurance policies. Or ask about local purchasing pools offering group rates to the self-employed at your state's insurance department or your local chamber of commerce. If you are self-employed, the National Association for the Self-Employed (NASE) also has a group policy; their phone number is 800-232-NASE.

If my neighbor's tree falls on my house and damages it, whose insurance covers the damage?

Your insurance company must pay for any trees that fall and damage your house, regardless of where the tree or tree limb comes from. (After all, in most storms it's hard to tell where fallen tree limbs came from.) Your insurer will pay for the cost of removing the tree as well as any damage it caused. In rare cases where a tree is definitely from a neighbor's property, your insurer may subrogate the claim to your neighbor's insurer. This just means that after your insurer has paid you, they may seek to recover damages from your neighbor's insurer. Neither you nor your neighbor will be involved in that process.

Do I need disability insurance after I retire?

Generally not. Theoretically, you shouldn't retire unless you have income sources in place to cover your current and future needs. (See pages 154-155 for more on retirement.) Since your costs are already covered, you don't need additional insurance. Besides, you probably wouldn't be able to get coverage since it's often based on how much you're earning.

Does liability insurance cover any lawsuits resulting from crimes committed by my child?

No. The personal umbrella liability policy usually excludes coverage for criminal or intentional illegal acts committed by you or any of your family members.

 ## HELPFUL RESOURCES

WEB SITES

www.insure.com

This consumer insurance site helps you research insurance issues and find answers to your insurance questions. Lots of handy tips, such as a list of car models that are most frequently stolen.

www.insweb.com

Offers free quotes for home, car, life, health, even pet insurance, from up to eight insurers.

www.acli.org

Consumer-oriented site for American Council of Life Insurance, a trade group. Helpful info on life insurance, disability, and long-term care.

www.napia.com

Site for the National Association of Public Insurance Adjusters. Includes names of adjusters near you.

www.iii.org

Insurance Information Institute's site. A non-profit organization that specializes in consumer information for auto, home, and business insurance.

BOOKS

Automobile Insurance Made Simple

by Ed Boylan, Mark Swercheck, Scott Weisel

The Complete Idiot's Guide to Buying Insurance and Annuities
by Brian H. Brevel

Life and Health Insurance
by Kenneth Black, Harold D. Skipper, Jr.

Taxes

7
TAXES

" Keep receipts and records of what you spend during the year. By keeping track of your expenses, you can find ways to cut your tax bill. "

understanding your taxes

Piecing together the puzzle

For many people, the thought of April 15th, when tax returns must be mailed to the Internal Revenue Service or IRS, unleashes a surge of anxious questions: How much do I owe? What can I deduct? Who gets what? Is there any way to pay less?

So let's simplify it: There are three taxes due on April 15: federal, state, and sometimes city taxes. Whatever you earned in the previous calendar year (January through December) you owe taxes on. In January, the IRS mails most taxpayers a booklet that contains federal income tax forms, instructions for filing, and **tax tables**—lists of taxes owed on all the different taxable income levels. (The exact forms they send depends on which forms you filed the year before.)

How do you know how much you owe in taxes? Here's a gross oversimplification: add up your W-2 income statements and 1099s, subtract your itemized deductions and personal exemptions and, voilà, you have your taxable income. Now look at the tax tables in the back of the tax booklet and find the amount of taxes you owe on it. If the right amount has been **withheld** from your paycheck (see page 10), you will owe the IRS nothing. If you withheld too much, you will get a **refund** from the IRS. If you didn't withhold enough, you will owe the IRS money. If you don't pay the difference on time, or intentionally pay less, you will have to pay a **penalty**, as well as **interest** on what you owe. That said, there are many ways you can lower your taxes. Read on and learn how.

Form W-4 (2002)

Purpose. Complete Form W-4 so your employer can withhold the correct Federal income tax from your pay. Because your tax situation may change, you may want to refigure your withholding each year.

Exemption from withholding. If you are exempt, complete only lines 1, 2, 3, 4, and 7 and sign the form to validate it. Your exemption for 2002 expires February 16, 2003. See **Pub. 505**, Tax Withholding and Estimated Tax.

Note: *You cannot claim exemption from withholding if (a) your income exceeds $750 and includes more than $250 of unearned income (e.g., interest and dividends) and (b) another person can claim you as a dependent on their tax return.*

Basic instructions. If you are not exempt, complete the **Personal Allowances Worksheet** below. The worksheets on page 2 adjust your withholding allowances based on itemized deductions, certain credits, adjustments to

income, or two-earner/tw[...]
plete all worksheets that [...]
may claim fewer (or zero [...]
Head of household. Gene [...]
head of household filing [...]
return only if you are unma [...]
than 50% of the costs of ke [...]
yourself and your dependen [...]
ing individuals. See line E bel [...]
Tax credits. You can take pr [...]
into account in figuring your a [...]
withholding allowances. Cred [...]
credit may be claimed using [...]
dependent care expenses ar [...]
Allowances Worksheet below. [...]
How Do I Adjust My Tax Withho [...]
mation on converting your oth [...]
withholding allowances.

Nonwage income. If you have a la [...]
nonwage income, such as interest [...]
consider making estimated tax pa [...]
Form 1040-ES, Estimated Tax fo [...]
Otherwise, you may owe additional t [...]

Personal Allowances Worksheet (Keep f[...]

A	Enter "1" for **yourself** if no one else can claim you as a dependent . . . . **A** _____
B	Enter "1" if: { • You are single and have only one job; or • You are married, have only one job, and your spouse does not work; or • Your wages from a second job or your spouse's wages (or the total of both) are $1,000 or less. } . . **B** _____
C	Enter "1" for your **spouse**. But, you may choose to enter "-0-" if you are married and have either a working spouse or more than one job. (Entering "-0-" may help you avoid having too little tax withheld.) . . . . . **C** _____
D	Enter number of **dependents** (other than your spouse or yourself) you will claim on your tax return . . . **D** _____
E	Enter "1" if you will file as **head of household** on your tax return (see conditions under **Head of household** above) . **E** _____
F	Enter "1" if you have at least $1,500 of **child or dependent care expenses** for which you plan to claim a credit . . **F** _____
	(Note: Do not include child support payments. See Pub. 503, Child and Dependent Care Expenses, for details.)
G	**Child Tax Credit** (including additional child tax credit):
	• If your total income will be between $15,000 and $42,000 ($20,000 and $65,000 if married), enter "1" for each eligible child plus 1 **additional** if you have three to five eligible children or **2 additional** if you have six or more eligible children.
	• If your total income will be between $42,000 and $80,000 ($65,000 and $115,000 if married), enter "1" if you have one or two eligible children, "2" if you have three eligible children, "3" if you have four eligible children, or "4" if you have five or more eligible children. **G** _____
H	Add lines A through G and enter total here. **Note:** *This may be different from the number of exemptions you claim on your tax return.* ▶ **H** _____

For accuracy, complete all worksheets that apply.	• If you plan to **itemize or claim adjustments to income** and want to reduce your withholding, see the **Deductions and Adjustments Worksheet** on page 2.	
	• If you have **more than one job** or are **married and you and your spouse both work** and the combined earnings from all jobs exceed $35,000, see the **Two-Earner/Two-Job Worksheet** on page 2 to avoid having too little tax withheld.	
	• If **neither** of the above situations applies, **stop here** and enter the number from line H on line 5 of Form W-4 below.	

Cut here and give Form W-4 to your employer. Keep the top part for your records.

Form **W-4** Department of the Treasury Internal Revenue Service	**Employee's Withholding Allowance Certificate** ▶ For Privacy Act and Paperwork Reduction Act Notice, see page 2.	OMB No. 1545-0010 20**02**

1	Type or print your first name and middle initial	Last name		2	Your social security number

Home address (number and street or rural route)	3 ☐ Single ☐ Married ☐ Married, but withhold at higher Single rate. **Note:** *If married, but legally separated, or spouse is a nonresident alien, check the "Single" box.*
City or town, state, and ZIP code	4 If your last name differs from that on your social security card, check here. You must call 1-800-772-1213 for a new card. ▶ ☐

5	Total number of allowances you are claiming (from line **H** above **or** from the applicable worksheet on page 2)	**5**	
6	Additional amount, if any, you want withheld from each paycheck	**6**	$
7	I claim exemption from withholding for 2002, and I certify that I meet **both** of the following conditions for exemption:		
	• Last year I had a right to a refund of **all** Federal income tax withheld because I had **no** tax liability **and**		
	• This year I expect a refund of **all** Federal income tax withheld because I expect to have **no** tax liability.		
	If you meet both conditions, write "Exempt" here . . . . ▶	**7**	

Under penalties of perjury, I certify that I am entitled to the number of withholding allowances claimed on this certificate, or I am entitled to claim exempt status.

Employee's signature
(Form is not valid
unless you sign it.) ▶ _____ Date ▶ _____

8	Employer's name and address (Employer: Complete lines 8 and 10 only if sending to the IRS.)	9 Office code (optional)	10 Employer identification number

---

W-2 Form

a Control number	22222	Void ☐	For Official Use Only ▶ OMB No. 1545-0008	

	1 Wages, tips, other compensation	2 Federal income tax withheld
b Employer identification number	$	$
	3 Social security wages	4 Social security tax withheld
c Employer's name, address, and ZIP code	$	$
	5 Medicare wages and tips	6 Medicare tax withheld
	$	$
	7 Social security tips	8 Allocated tips
	$	$
	9 Advance EIC payment	10 Dependent care benefits
	$	$
d Employee's social security number	11 Nonqualified plans	12a See instructions for box 12
	$	$
e Employee's first name and initial Last name	13 Statutory employee ☐ Retirement plan ☐ Third-party sick pay ☐	12b $
	14 Other	12c $
		12d $
f Employee's address and ZIP code		
15 State Employer's state ID number	16 State wages, tips, etc. $	17 State income tax $
	18 Local wages, tips, etc. $	19 Local income tax $	20 Locality name

Form W-2 **Wage and Tax Statement** (99)   **2002**
(Rev. February 2002)   Cat. No. 10134D

Department of the Treasury—Internal Revenue Service
For Privacy Act and Paperwork Reduction Act Notice, see separate instructions.

Copy A For Social Security Administration—Send this entire page with Form W-3 to the Social Security Administration; photocopies are **not** acceptable.

Do Not Cut, Fold, or Staple Forms on This Page — Do Not Cut, Fold, or Staple Forms on This Page

---

How do you know how much you made in the past calendar year? Well, sometime in January you receive W-2 wage and tax statements. These are tax forms stating how much money you made during the year. The amount of money withheld is based on the number of allowances you claim on the W-4 form (a form you filled out when you were hired).

keeping records

*File now,
smile later*

Here's a really simple way to save money on taxes: keep receipts and records of what you spend during the year. Most people don't realize how items such as gas for business trips add up. By keeping track of your expenses, you can find ways to cut your tax bill.

First, create three big folders for these tax-related categories:
Income: Here's where you put your W-2 forms, 1099s, brokerage statements, bank statements, receipts of rental property income, any pension distributions, and other forms of income.

Adjustments to Gross Income: In this file put any bills related to moving, statements about any IRA contributions you made, alimony payments, and if you are self-employed, your self-employment medical insurance receipts and SEP contributions.

Deductions: This can be one big file or you can break it up into separate folders to cover: medical expenses; taxes—the amount paid for state and local income taxes as well as your property tax; mortgage interest; margin or investment interest, casualty losses, charity donations; and any miscellaneous and job-related expenses.

SK THE EXPERTS

How long am I supposed to hold on to my piles of tax receipts and records?

Seven years is long enough. While the statute of limitations for tax audits is three years, the IRS actually can call you up to six years later if they think you underpaid. (They can pester you even longer if they think they can prove tax fraud.) As you add tax records for each year, remove the oldest one of the seven you are holding. Before you discard anything, look for files you will need to keep over the long-term, particularly information on expenses and improvements related to your home or other real estate you own. Those costs can be deductible if and when you sell the property—which could be years from now.

When will the records I need be coming in the mail?

Keep an eye out in January for *year-end statements* such as your last paycheck stub. It lists how much you donated to charity at work, how much you paid for medical insurance premiums and union dues, and how much was deducted for your 401(k). In January and February, you'll start getting forms and other year-end statements. Your year-end brokerage statement is valuable. Also, look out for your W-2 forms (your employer's report of how much you earned the previous year and how much you paid in taxes); 1098s (reporting how much mortgage interest you paid); and 1099s (reporting stock sales, dividends and investment income, earnings as an independent contractor, or distributions from retirement plans).

I know myself. There's no way I will keep to an organized system. What can I do?

If you're not the file-folder type and you don't use personal finance software (see page 22), just pile up the mail as it comes in, and set aside some time after the first of the year when you can go into hyperdrive and attack that pile.

Bring organized records—not tote bags bursting with unopened receipts and statements—when you visit a tax adviser. This way you pay her to focus on ways to save you money, not to sort through your mess.

preparing a return

It could pay you to start early

First, estimate your gross income. Simply add up all sources of income, such as wages, tips, bonus, severance pay, unemployment compensation, interest on your bank accounts and investments, dividends, lottery or gambling winnings, and alimony. Second, add up any **adjustments** you can make, such as IRA contributions. Next estimate your **deductions**. You can use the **standard deduction**—the amount the IRS figures an average taxpayer with your income racks up in deductible expenses in a year. Or you can use the total of an "itemized" list of **itemized deductions** you're entitled to, such as mortgage interest, a percentage of your medical expenses, and certain losses from investments (see page 140).

Finally, subtract your **exemptions**. For the tax year 2002, the amount is $3,000 for you personally and the same for each of your dependents. **Dependents** include any relative for whom you provide over 50% of their financial support, e.g., children, elderly parents, Great-Aunt Larissa.

What's left is your taxable income. Ah, but exactly how is it taxed, you ask. Well, here's some good news: everyone is taxed at the lowest income bracket first. What's leftover is taxed at the next highest bracket, on and on until your income maxes out at the 38.6% bracket for any net income over $307,051. The tax brackets below list the income ranges.

TAX BRACKETS FOR 2002

The higher your income, the more a portion of it will be taxed at a higher percentage tax bracket. Luckily, your income figure can be lowered by exemptions and deductions before it is taxed. Here are some tax bracket examples:

Tax rate	Single	Married (filing jointly)
10%	$0 to $6,000	$0 to $12,000
15%	$6,001 to $27,950	$12,001 to $46,700
27%	$27,951 to $67,700	$46,701 to $112,850
30%	$67,701 to $141,250	$112,851 to $171,950
35%	$141,251 to $307,050	$171,951 to $307,050
38.6%	over $307,051	over $307,051

ASK THE EXPERTS

What does filing "jointly" mean?

The term refers to one method used by married couples to pay taxes with their combined incomes. This is different from "married, filing separately" where each spouse files his and her own separate return. Ask an accountant to analyze your situation to see if it is advantageous for you and your spouse to file jointly or separately. In most cases, filing jointly is better.

Who is considered a "head of household"?

This refers to an unmarried person who maintains a household for at least one child or grandchild. You don't have to provide financial support, just maintain the home for your dependents in order to qualify for this advantageous rate.

I'm self-employed. How and when do I pay taxes?

Since no one is withholding your income taxes during the year, you have to pay estimated taxes every three months. First you figure out how much tax you think you'll owe. You can base it on your previous year's income and then divide it by four. Or base it on the net earnings of the prior three months. Whichever figure you use, you are responsible for paying this amount every three months. You need to get the IRS form 1040-ES, and mark your calendar: payments are due the 15th of the month in April, June, September, and the following January. (Okay, so it's not exactly quarterly.) People who live in an area that has state and/or city income taxes need to make those estimated payments at the same time. If you make more during one quarter than the last, you can make up for it on the next quarterly payment, or you can wait until the following April when you send in your annual income tax return.

What happens if I forget to pay a quarterly estimated tax payment?

You'll be delinquent, which can result in interest charges and possible fines. (Read "Easing the Pain.")

EASING THE PAIN

To make sure you have the money on hand for quarterly payments, it is smart to "withhold" your tax money as an employer does. Set aside a percentage of each income check you receive, perhaps by putting it in a savings account. Then don't touch it until it's time to pay the quarterlies.

look for deductions and credits

These everyday expenses can add up!

Uncle Sam gives everyone a standard deduction, just for paying taxes. If you don't wish to itemize your deductions, then subtract the amount the IRS gives you. In the year 2002, you get to deduct $4,700 if you're single, $7,850 if you and your spouse are filing jointly (on the same form with income combined), $6,900 if you're head of a household, and $3,925 each if you and your spouse file separately (you file your own separate returns with only your own income and expenses on each one). Don't think that covers all the deductible expenses you had for the year? Then you can **itemize** each and every deduction. Why itemize? Most likely your deductions will add up to more than the standard deduction and you'll pay less in taxes. A list of common deductions appears on pages 138-139.

There are even faster ways to reduce your tax bill—through tax credits. While a deduction reduces your taxable income, a credit directly reduces your tax bill. In other words, if you owe $5,000 in taxes and you qualify for $600 in **tax credits**, you end up owing $4,400. So grab whatever tax credits you can. A list of major tax credits appears on page 139.

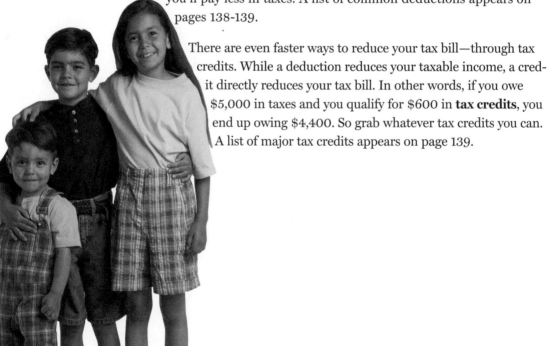

ASK THE EXPERTS

I'm always running around on April 14 to get my tax return together. But my brother simply files an extension. Can I do this?

Sure, anyone can file an extension—all you need to do is ask for (and fill out) Form 4868. The IRS will grant you another four months to get the paperwork done. But even with an extension, you must go ahead and pay your taxes by April 15 or you will owe interest and penalties. And make sure your extension request is postmarked by April 15th. Otherwise you'll owe the usual late-filing payment of 5% for every month that you are late, up to a maximum of 5 months or 25%. Yikes!

Each year, I go to the tax storefront, wait an hour, then hand over a fee of $100 and my paperwork. It takes the preparer all of 15 minutes to fill out my return. Is it really that simple?

It's probably easy enough to do yourself if:

- You're single, or you're married, filing jointly
- You have no dependents
- You don't itemize your deductions
- Your taxable annual income is less than $50,000
- You made less than $400 in interest income

If you meet all these requirements, skip the tax preparer's office and just fill out form 1040EZ—about a dozen lines long. Send in a check or wait for your refund, depending on your situation. (And if you contributed to an IRA, but you still meet all other qualifications, you can use a 1040A form, which is almost as simple.)

I have heard the term "adjusted gross income." What does it mean?

It's also referred to as AGI, and it is gross income that's been "adjusted" by subtracting the following: IRA contributions (see page 156), moving expenses, alimony, the interest penalties on withdrawal from savings and CD accounts, student loan interest; and if you are self-employed, any retirement plans, half of your self-employment tax, and 70% of your medical insurance (100% starting with 2003 returns).

60 SECONDS $ SAVINGS

Expecting a refund? Tell the IRS to deposit your refund directly into your bank account. You'll get the money faster, and you'll be less likely to spend it if it never goes through your hands. Just fill out the section on your tax form that asks for your bank account number.

Common deductions and tax credits

ITEMIZED DEDUCTIONS

These are subtracted directly from your adjusted gross income before you figure your taxes. If the following deductions add up to more than the standard deduction, you will save money on taxes by itemizing your deductions.

Mortgage interest: Interest you pay on the mortgage for your home and vacation home is deductible, as well as interest on a home equity loan (on up to $100,000 in borrowings). You can also deduct the closing points you pay on the mortgage for your primary residence.

Margin or Investment interest: You get to deduct any investment interest you might have incurred in your brokerage account or on other investment loans, up to the amount of your total investment income. This is interest money you paid out to your broker or a bank to purchase investments.

Taxes: Deduct state, county, or city income taxes; real estate property taxes; and certain personal property taxes.

Donations: Contributions (cash and non-cash) to tax-exempt organizations are fully deductible. Just be sure to document everything. Note: if a non-cash gift is over $500, you need to file form 8283 that details the item and records which charity you gave it to.

DEDUCTIONS: 10%

Add together all the losses from a disaster, casualty, or theft.

Casualty losses: If your house is washed away in a flood, or part of it burns down, or if a burglar loots your belongings, there may be some compensation from Uncle Sam. You are allowed to deduct the uninsured part of any disaster, casualty, or theft loss that exceeds 10% of your AGI. If the loss was in a disaster area that has been federally declared as such, you may qualify for other tax breaks, too.

DEDUCTIONS: 7.5%

Add together all medical expenses that are not covered by insurance.

Medical expenses: You can deduct out-of-pocket medical costs for you and your dependents that exceed 7.5% of your AGI. That might sound insurmountable until you realize all the items that count: co-payments; deductibles; insurance premiums; psychological counseling; dental and chiropractic services (the amount not covered by medical plans); eyeglasses; transportation to and from the health provider; certain driving devices or home improvements for the disabled; and doctor-recommended programs to lose weight, stop drinking, or stop smoking (including travel to a 12-step group).

Note: If one year you have a large medical bill which is more than 7.5% of your adjusted gross income, add more medical expenses to it, because you'll be able to deduct them completely. For instance, get that extra pair of reading glasses or contact lenses; join a weight loss program; or get that bum knee fixed that you've been putting off doing. Remember you only get to deduct the amount that exceeds 7.5% of your adjusted gross income. If you have $3,800 in medical expenses with an adjusted gross income of $50,000, you can only write off $50. (7.5% of $50,000 is $3,750.)

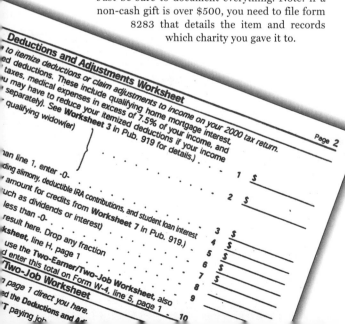

DEDUCTIONS: 2%

Add together the following miscellaneous deductions. You get to deduct the amount that exceeds 2% of your adjusted gross income. Miscellaneous deductions include:

Education: If you enroll in classes or training related to your line of work, your costs for tuition, books, and travel are deductible. (That is, unless your employer reimburses you.) But here's the caveat: courses have to further your current line of work. If you want to be a rocket scientist and you're currently a chef, such expenses aren't deductible.

Unreimbursed career advancement expenses: If you're employed in New York state, and you're considering a job in New Mexico, you can deduct expenses related to interviewing, even if you don't take the job. In fact, job search expenses are deductible in general, as long as you are moving within your field. But if you are changing careers, you can't deduct the expenses.

Career expenses: Costs related to your job that your employer doesn't pay for, such as trade journal subscriptions, uniforms or other specialty clothing (including the cleaning expenses), union dues, tools the boss makes you buy, travel, entertaining and other expenses your job requires (like a passport fee), a cell phone, and miles you log doing your job (other than for your commute).

Financial expenses: What you spend on money-making goods or services are deductible. This includes fees for your financial planner or accountant; subscriptions to newsletters, magazines, and books about investing (including this one!); your safe deposit box; certain investment seminars that teach you about taxable income (a seminar on tax-free bonds wouldn't cut it, for example); software and on-line services to help you follow your investments.

MOST COMMON TAX CREDITS

These can be deducted directly from your tax bill if your adjusted gross income meets certain qualifications:

Child and dependent care credit: This covers some of what you paid for qualified child or dependent care, such as babysitting, nurseries, or elder care while you are at work. Some caveats: the kids have to be under age 13, and older dependents must be unable to care for themselves. The credit can cover no more than 30% of what you paid, and the amount paid can't exceed $2,400 per dependent, or $4,800 total. You must list the care provider's Tax I.D. or Social Security number, or you don't get the credit.

Child credit: Reduce your taxes by $600 for each child you have who is a dependent, under age 17, and is a U.S. citizen. (You must include the child's Social Security number; otherwise you don't get the credit.)

Adoption credit: When you adopt a child, you may qualify for a credit of $10,000.

College credits: For the first two years of college, the Hope Scholarship Credit allows you to take a credit equal to the first $1,000 you spend on tuition and other college expenses and 50 cents on the dollar for the next $1,000, up to $1,500 each year for up to two years. The student (you, your spouse, or dependent) has to attend college at least half-time, for at least one semester. After the first two years of college, another tax credit called the Lifetime Learning Credit picks up where the Hope Credit leaves off. For each student take a tax credit equal to 20% of the first $5,000 of college expenses.

using tax software

Bet Uncle Sam never dreamed of E-tax filing

Tax preparation software can save you tons of time filling out tax forms—especially if you decide to take advantage of on-line tax filing. Moreover, each new year's software contains the latest tax code changes as well as tax breaks for which you might not have known you qualify. And it also provides all the forms you need, so there's no more running around getting that obscure form you need before you can file. Best of all, you can even use it to file your federal returns via the Internet.

Two popular tax software programs are Quicken's TurboTax and Kiplinger's TaxCut. Both come with helpful tricks to make filing a breeze. TurboTax has video clips of a real person explaining tax concepts in real English. TaxCut comes with tax tips from the financial experts at *Kiplinger's* magazine.

With the programs, once you have finished entering all the information, you can review it for errors, overlooked deductions, and audit alerts. In addition, you can create a customized action plan to help reduce your taxes in the future. When you are ready, you can print your tax return and mail it in, or simply E-mail it.

TurboTax®is tax preparation software that includes video clips of a real person explaining tax concepts in plain English so they are easy to understand. If you have trouble hearing the tax lady, your computer's sound level may be too low. Turn up the volume by clicking on your control panel and then selecting sound. You should see a volume control feature you can adjust with your mouse.

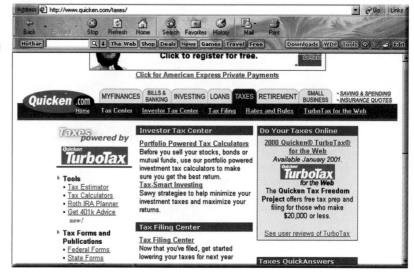

 HAT IF

You want to download IRS forms?

If you log on to the Internal Revenue Service Web site at **www.irs.gov**, you can download IRS forms and follow links to state forms. Choose from either Electronic Services or Forms & Pubs.

You want to file your taxes on-line?

You can use your tax preparation software to file on-line—the tax preparation software uses an electronic filing center to transmit your encrypted tax data securely over the Internet. Keep in mind that not all states allow electronic filing. Check to see if yours does.

If you've downloaded your IRS forms from the Internet, you can use the IRS Web site to file on-line after you choose from one of the filing companies they have listed. Don't go with a filing company unless it is IRS approved. Your on-line return might not be accepted. Note: The IRS does not post the names of the filing companies until the first of January each year.

You want to find unbiased tax advice?

Visit TaxWeb at **www.irs.com**, which provides links to dozens of Web sites that offer tax-related discussion groups, federal and state tax sites, and tax software developers.

RED●FLAG

HELP! I NEED SOMEBODY

If you need help understanding something in Turbo-Tax, click the Help button at any time. You can look at frequently asked questions, obtain tax help, review government instructions, read IRS publications, peruse the **Money Income Tax Handbook,** check out the video library, or go through tax questions and answers.

getting tax help

The ABCs of working with CPAs and other tax professionals

If you're uncomfortable doing your own taxes, or you just don't have the time, or your return is too complicated for you to deal with, find a professional to help you. But find someone well before tax season, as many are bound to be booked come spring. Some good news: A tax preparer's fee might be tax deductible. Here's a list of the type of help available:

Unlicensed tax preparers: These are typically financial planners, or independent specialists who work in storefront tax centers and fill out returns on a part-time basis. If all you need is someone to fill in a few forms, go with this, the least expensive option. Preparers don't have to meet educational requirements beyond what their employer calls for. Please note, however, they can't represent you in the event of an audit. They charge about $100 or so, depending on the return.

Enrolled agents: They're certified by the IRS (in fact, many have been IRS auditors). If your return is a bit challenging, consider this alternative. They can represent you in audits and hearings, and are required to further their education in tax preparation each year. They charge more than preparers but less than CPAs, usually $200 per return. For more information, call their national organization at 800-424-4339 or look online at **www.naea.org**.

Certified public accountants (CPA): These are often the best-informed tax advisors. They're licensed by the state and must meet training and continuing education requirements. You pay for all this expertise, of course. CPAs typically charge $125-$250 an hour, or even more, depending on the work involved and the complexity of the return. They are good for people who are freelancers or own their own businesses. To find a CPA in your area, call their national association, American Institute of CPAs at 888-777-7077 or go to their Web site **AICPA.org**.

Tax attorneys: These are expensive experts who are needed by people with very complicated tax returns or those who have legal issues, such as a divorce.

STEP BY STEP: HIRING THE RIGHT TAX ADVISORS

1. Ask your colleagues, family, and friends for recommendations of tax professionals they have used. Call and find out about their credentials. Ask how many of their clients file an extension. (You don't need an overworked person trying to squeeze you in.) Ask how much they charge to prepare returns. Ask, too, if they offer a guarantee. Any preparer worth her weight in forms will pay interest or penalties caused by errors she commits. There's no need to feel intimidated about asking such questions.

2. Narrow your list to a couple of finalists and interview them in person. Find out if their expertise matches your needs. For example, if you run your own business, work on the road, or you have holdings or do business in another state, you want an advisor who knows how to handle your deductions. Take a couple of your most recent tax returns along to discuss.

3. Once you have decided on a tax preparer, ask how she wants your information to be presented. For instance, she may want to look at several of your past returns. She may give you a form to help you gather the figures or receipts she needs from you. As you prepare your records, try to make notes about points that concern you, so that you can ask any pertinent questions while she has your information handy.

4. When your return is completed, review all the numbers carefully before signing and mailing them. If there's something amiss in your return, you are liable—even if the accountant signed her name alongside yours.

tax-smart investing

It starts with free money from the boss

Investing is a great way to earn money, but it comes at a price: taxes. You get taxed on the profit you make (called a **capital gains tax**), as well as dividends and interest you earn, which are treated as regular income. There are two types of capital gains tax: short- and long-term. Short-term capital tax applies to profit on investments that are sold within one year of their purchase. The tax rate for short-term capital gains, as well as interest and dividends, is taxed at the tax bracket you are in. If you hold onto your investment for longer than a year and then sell, you will be taxed on your profit at only 10% or 20%, depending on the tax bracket you are in.

One of the smartest ways to save on taxes also happens to be one of the smartest ways to save for your retirement. It's called tax-deferred investing. It's where the income you earn on investments

is not taxed until after your retirement, when you are most likely to be in a lower tax bracket.

Retirement plans such as 401(k)s and 403(b)s let you stash away some pay before it gets recorded as income, so you don't pay current income taxes on it (see page 70). Your employer may match some of your contribution, giving you additional income, also tax-deferred at this point. If your company doesn't offer a retirement plan, you and your spouse can contribute $2,000 apiece, tax-deferred, to an individual retirement account (IRA) or a Roth IRA (see page 71). Taxes are deferred until you withdraw funds during retirement when you are most likely to be in a lower tax bracket.

Another tax-smart investment is to buy a home, and if you can afford it, a vacation home. Uncle Sam likes real estate. In fact, he lets you deduct your mortgage interest, as well as points you may pay at the closing of your primary home (see page 138).

Ask THE EXPERTS

Does an investment's tax status matter all that much?

It sure does. Suppose you're in the 30% tax bracket, you received a $20,000 gift, and you lumped the whole thing into a CD (see page 45) earning 5% interest. (You're saving—that's a good start.) On paper, you generate $1,000 in interest in a year—but Uncle Sam will snag $300 of it. On the other hand, if you put the money in a tax-free investment that earns only 4%, such as a municipal bond (see page 95), you won't pay a dime of federal tax, but you'll end up with more money.

Can I deduct any losses from my taxes?

Yes, it's called a **capital loss**. Here's how it works: if you sell an investment for less than you bought it for, you have a capital loss. After you combine that loss with any capital gains made in a tax year, any losses you have left over, up to $3,000, can be deducted from your other income.

Am I always better off with a tax-friendly investment?

Not necessarily. You actually could earn less than you'd get after paying taxes on a regular investment. To determine which is better for you, figure out your "after-tax" rate of return on the taxable investment. Here's how:

1. Convert your tax bracket into a decimal. If you are in the 27% tax bracket, then the number you want is .27.

2. Subtract that from the "pre-tax" rate of return on your investment, let's say it's 9%. On a calculator, punch in .09, then multiply it by .27. You should get .024. Now hit the minus key and then punch in .09 and you should get .066. That translates into a 6.6% after-tax rate of return.

60 SECONDS $ SAVINGS

Making donations count in more ways than one

■ **Money donations:** Get receipts for cash, or for checks for $250 or more (the IRS doesn't accept as documentation canceled checks for $250 or more).

■ **Travel and transportation:** List the destinations, dates, and miles you log doing good deeds, as you can deduct 14 cents a mile for your volunteering efforts. (Helping the old lady across town doesn't qualify. Only work for tax-exempt charities does.)

■ **Stocks:** Say you paid $1,000 for 50 shares of Hotstock.com more than a year ago, and now they're worth $4,000. If you sell the stocks you have to pay federal capital gains tax of 20% on your net profit. But, depending on your AGI, if you donate the stock instead of selling it, you can deduct the full $4,000.

■ **Goods:** Go through the clothes, toys, sports gear, or computer equipment gathering dust in your closet. Take it to Goodwill, the Salvation Army, a homeless shelter, or other charitable group. The IRS will let you deduct the fair-market value (how much the goods are likely to be resold for).

■ **Expensive goods:** For anything valued over $5,000, such as works of art, antiques, collections, or real estate, get a formal appraisal when you donate it. File the amount on federal form 8283, part 2.

dealing with an audit

Give them what they want and no more

If the IRS does come knocking, keep calm. Never, ever, ignore the notices. The instant you're notified, respond—even if it's just to ask for a postponement to gather your records. If your deductions are complicated or questionable (or if you're just plain terrified), get help from the only people allowed to represent you in an audit: a tax attorney, a CPA, or an enrolled agent. If possible, use the one who helped you prepare your taxes; he will be familiar with everything.

There are three categories of audits, each one progressively more exhaustive. Most people fall into the least intrusive: the **correspondence audit** category, in which the IRS sends you a notice asking for more information on a couple of items. You send them copies of the information, and you're done. (Granted, this is after you get to spend a week in your basement digging up two- or three-year-old tax return information.)

If the IRS has questions that are more serious, you will be asked to meet with an examiner in your district for an **office audit**. In this case, bring only the information they're asking about. Get as familiar with it as you can, because you will need to explain it precisely. Don't tell them your whole life story. In fact, don't volunteer any information. Usually your tax preparer will accompany you. If you don't have one, contact one, and get his or her advice before you go.

On the most serious occasions there is the **field audit**, where IRS agents come to your home(s) to scrutinize your lifestyle up close and personal. They want to see if your tax return makes sense in light of your reported income. In this case, if your his-and-hers Porsches sit in the garage as you and your mate lounge by the pool, jointly claiming a $40,000 income, it's usually too late to do much except hire a good lawyer.

ASK THE EXPERTS

I think we can take certain deductions, but my husband is afraid that if we do we'll get audited. What should we do?

It helps to run the items in question by a tax advisor, at least the first time you claim a given deduction, or if you are claiming quite a bit more than usual. If you do your own taxes, don't let the fear of an audit stop you from taking the deductions to which you're entitled. Simply keep a solid paper trail so you can support everything you deduct. The more thorough your records, the easier to defend your return.

What if the auditors disallow my claims?

If the auditor tells you to pay up, or denies your claims, and you disagree, don't grovel or whimper. On the other hand, don't cause a scene. Just calmly support your contentions and make it clear that you intend to defend yourself as far as you can. Then ask to see the auditor's supervisor. If you don't get a satisfactory response from the supervisor, call your tax advisor for advice. If he tells you that you have a good case, and the amount in question is less than $10,000, ask the auditor to bring it before the IRS Internal Appeals Unit. On the other hand, if a reputable tax lawyer says your claim is iffy, weigh your options carefully before you proceed. There will be costly penalties and interest if you lose.

The IRS is challenging a deduction I took. I have three months to respond; meanwhile they are charging me interest on what I owe. Is that legal?

Yes, it is. That's how the IRS gets your attention. If you think they are right about a tax issue, then pay up immediately. Contesting can be costly in terms of interest and penalties you may owe if you lose.

HELP! I NEED SOMEBODY

You can't avoid a random audit, but you can make sure your return doesn't stand out. Try to avoid raising any of these red flags:

- Married, filing separately, with mismatched expenses on the two returns
- Refunds higher than the average for your gross income and exemptions
- Work that offers the possibility of unreported income, such as bartending or landscaping
- Donating more to charity than seems typical for your income
- Donations other than cash

now what do I do?

Answers to common questions

When should I send in my tax return?

Your employers and financial institutions are required to send out your annual financial forms by January 31. If you're due a refund, submit your return as soon as possible after you receive your forms. The earlier you send in the return, the less time it takes the IRS to process it—and the sooner you can put your refund to work. If you owe money, though, you might as well let it work for you as long as possible. Sending in your check by April 15 will accomplish that. The envelope your tax forms are mailed in must bear a postmark no later than April 15. Be sure to put enough postage on the envelope; if it is returned, you will face a penalty for late filing.

I'm always running all over town trying to find the tax forms I need. Any suggestions?

It's true, the stacks of forms at the library or post office may have dwindled just when you need them most. If you have some leeway in your schedule, call the IRS at 800-TAX-FORM to have them mail the ones you want. If you have a computer at home or at work, or access to one at the library, all the forms are just a click away on-line. Download them from the Web site **www.irs.gov**.

How do I deduct for my home office? And what exactly can I deduct?

You need to file Form 8829 along with your tax return. What can you deduct? If your place of business is a room in your home used only for your work, you can deduct the associated costs, including furniture, phone lines, and computer, as well as a percentage of your heating, utilities, and insurance. (Remember, keep receipts for all expenses you claim.) There are two ways to calculate the portion of your home attributed to your office: by square footage or by number of rooms. For example, if you have a 5-room house and one room is for your home office, then you can deduct 20% of your heating, utilities, and insurance.

I get a nice tax refund each year. My sister says that's not a good thing. Why not?

If you get a refund, it means the government has had more of your money during the year than it should have. That's bad news for you because—surprise—the government isn't going to pay you any interest on that money it's been using. If you had the money you could have been saving it in an interest-bearing account. So it's important to make sure you are not having extra money withheld.

Is Social Security taxable?

Sometimes. Depending on what other income you have to include, anywhere from zero to 85% of your Social Security could be taxed. You need to use a special worksheet to figure out how much is tax free. Don't worry, it's included in the tax booklet.

I know my tax bill is going to be high this year due to some unexpected income. How can I cut down on the extra taxes?

If you know your income is going to be particularly high one year, try to pay more deductible expenses that year to offset the extra income. For example, double your contributions to your house of worship or favorite charity in the high-income year, and skip them the next. Another good idea: pay your January mortgage in December.

Ⓗ ELPFUL RESOURCES

WEB SITES	BOOKS
www.hrblock.com/taxes To download tax forms and locate H&R Block offices near you.	**Taxes for Dummies** by David J. Silverman and Eric Tyson
www.irs.gov The IRS Web site. Go there to download any tax forms you need.	**Kiplinger's Cut Your Taxes** by Kevin McCormally
www.irs.com For information about your state's tax laws, forms, and filing info.	**J.K. Lasser's Your Income Tax** by J.K. Lasser Institute
www.quickfinders.com For information about taxes and financial planning.	

Retirement

8

RETIREMENT

" The good news is that you don't have to save for retirement all by yourself. Uncle Sam, your employer, and possibly the stock market can help. "

help with retirement

It's not so scary when you consider the help you'll get

The good news is that you don't have to save for retirement all by yourself. Uncle Sam, your employer, and possibly the stock market can help. Before you figure out how much to save, find out what may already be coming to you when you retire.

■ First, figure out how much money you will receive every month from **Social Security** when you turn a certain age, usually anywhere from 62 to 67, depending on your birth year. (This is a federal government program that was created back in 1935 under the Federal Insurance Contributions Act or FICA to help support people when they retire.) You are already contributing to it, since a part of every paycheck goes to the program. Take a look at the FICA deduction on your next paycheck (see page 11). You can call Social Security and they will tell you the projected amount you will receive upon retirement. The number is 800-772-1213. Just ask for a personal earnings and benefits statement (or a PEBES). Or order one on-line at Social Security's Web site: **www.ssa.gov**

■ Second, find out if your employer has a **pension plan**—that's a plan that gives you a set amount of money each year when you retire, based on the number of years you worked. If your company has a pension plan, ask your employee benefits department to help you figure out what your annual pension payments might be.

■ Third, check out your company's **defined contribution plan,** also known as a **401(k) plan.** (If you work for a non-profit firm or public agency, it's a 403(b) plan.) See page 71 for more info. Here you contribute a fixed percentage of your salary every paycheck to the plan. Your employer takes the money and invests it for you in a tax-deferred account. Some companies even match your contributions dollar for dollar. Talk about found money! You pay no taxes on 401(k) funds, or their earnings, until you withdraw them during retirement.

ASK THE EXPERTS

What if I work for myself?

There are essentially two retirement savings plans you can set up for yourself. The simplest is the SEP IRA (see page 71). It lets you contribute 20% of your net business income or $40,000, whichever is less. The other is the SIMPLE plan, which is suitable if you're a small business owner and want to contribute on your employees' behalf.

What happens if I change jobs?

You can move your funds to your new employer's 401(k), or leave them at your old job. The most common action is to "roll over" your account into an IRA. Either way, you get the money when you retire, and until then, it keeps earning tax-deferred interest.

What if my company doesn't have a 401(k)?

Consider using a traditional IRA or Roth IRA (see page 71). You can open an IRA at a bank, brokerage house, or mutual fund company, and contribute up to $3,000 ($6,000 for married couples) annually—tax deferred. Or you can contribute to a Roth IRA if you make less than $95,000 ($150,000 for married couples). Roths are not tax deductible when you contribute, but are tax free when you withdraw money at retirement.

What if I need my money before I retire?

You can "borrow" money from your 401(k). And like any other loan, you have to pay interest on it. (The only good news here is that you get to pay yourself the interest.) If you don't pay it back, however, you will be taxed on it and possibly penalized. If you have your money in an IRA account or a SEP IRA account, there is a 10% penalty, in addition to taxes, for taking the money out before you turn 59 1/2. You're also allowed to make a one-time penalty-free withdrawal of $10,000 from your IRA account if it's toward the purchase of a first home. The money is taxed when you withdraw it, though.

how much will I need to retire?

To avoid trouble, ask yourself this question early in your career

RETIREMENT CALCULATORS

An easy way to estimate how much you'll need to save is to use a **retirement calculator**. It takes all your numbers, factors in inflation and gives you the amount you need to save. There are many on the Web. Three good calculators can be found at:

www.money.cnn.com
www.kiplinger.com
www.quicken.com

A couple of ballpark examples: If you're earning $40,000 now and want the same standard of living after you retire, you'd want to save about 8% of your earnings a year if you're 25; 16% if you're 35; and—this is admittedly tough—36% if you're 45. (That's $11,110 a year you would need to sock away.)

Don't let anyone sell you on some magic figure. How much you'll need depends on the lifestyle you want to have. If you're like most people, you'll need 80% of your annual pre-retirement income to maintain your same standard of living. Why only 80%? Well, the theory is that some of your **expenses** (your monthly costs, such as clothes and transportation) will be less. For example, you won't need such a large wardrobe if you're not going to the office every day, and your commuting costs will be a thing of the past. Chances are that you will have paid off the mortgage on your house or condo.

The magic number is not necessarily how much you need to retire, but how much you need to save. $1,000 a year? $2,000 a year? $10,000 a year? The amount you need to save will depend not on how disciplined you are, but rather how old you are. The earlier you start, the less you'll need to put away because of the wonders of **compound interest**—where you earn interest on interest. The longer your retirement fund has to grow, the bigger it gets. For example, if a 25-year-old saves $2,000 every year in a retirement account earning 10%, she'll have $1 million when she turns 65. A 35-year-old who does the same thing, will have $377,000 when she turns 65. Now how about a 45-year-old? She would have $127,000 when she turns 65. (Simple math tells you that she would need to save much more to reach $1 million in 20 years than 40 years.)

If you haven't saved a dime for your retirement, you are not alone. It's never too late to start to save; and if you invest your savings wisely (see page 67), they will grow substantially.

HIDDEN RETIREMENT COSTS

There are a number of things to juggle when you are figuring out your retirement needs. Two "invisible" things to consider right away: inflation (see page 65) and taxes (see page 128). These two bugaboos will eat into what you will be living on in the future so you need to factor in their effect. Experts suggest figuring on a 4% rate of inflation; and a 15% to 28% tax rate. Put those two figures together and that means that if your 401(k) or IRA is worth $100,000 today and it doesn't earn a dime in 20 years, after taxes at 25% and inflation at 4% you'll only have enough money to buy about $34,000 worth of goods and services in today's dollars. Ouch!

FIRST PERSON   DISASTER STORY

Home Sweet Home Again

When my husband and I retired three years ago, we decided to sell our house in Connecticut and move to a golfing community in North Carolina. We thought we'd be able to live on half the money we'd spent up north. After all, we'd have no commuting costs and a smaller house so our bills would be much smaller. Boy, were we wrong! We hadn't added in the costs of our new community: first the dues on the golf course doubled the first year because they wanted to expand the club house, then our electric bill was astronomical because the house had electric heat and we didn't know just how cold it can get in North Carolina. Second, we missed our family and friends and flew up more than we thought we would. Finally, after two years, we realized we were spending more than we had planned for and moved back to a smaller house in our home town in Connecticut. Now we are getting ourselves back on better financial footing. If only we had investigated our retirement move a little more.

Nancy M., Bethel, Connecticut

retiring right

As you get ready to retire, you need to get your financial house in order. This means changing your mindset from that of a saver/investor to that of a spender. Why? Because when you retire, it's time for the money you've been investing to be used as income for you to live on. Financial advisors recommend that about five years before you retire, you start moving some of your money out of stocks and bonds and into less risky investments, such as money market accounts. You can't risk losing money in the stock market if you need it to live on.

You also need to plan when and how you will cash out any retirment accounts such as IRAs and 401(k)s. There are different withdrawal rules for each retirement plan. If you take the money out too soon or too late, you could get hit with a tax penalty that you must pay.

Here are the general withdrawal guidelines:

401(k): You can take money from your 401(k) starting at age 55, as long as you've left the company—but taking it out all at once could put you in an ultra-high tax bracket for the year.

IRA: You can withdraw IRA funds starting at the age of 59 1/2. (If you withdraw any of it earlier you face a 10% tax penalty.) Once you reach 70 1/2, you must start withdrawing your IRA money by April 1st of the following year or you will be hit with a 50% tax penalty on the amount you were supposed to take out.

Roth IRA: You can start to withdraw Roth money when you turn 59 1/2 or at any time thereafter, as much or as little as you want. There is no withdrawal requirement when you become 70 1/2 years old. This is a good vehicle for leaving funds to your heirs.

Social Security: Payments begin according to your birth year. (Check the chart on the opposite page.)

ASK THE EXPERTS

When should I apply for Social Security benefits?

You should apply for Social Security at least three months before you turn 65. Telephone 800-772-1213 to arrange it. If you need money before age 65, you can apply for Social Security starting at age 62, but your payments will be up to 20% smaller. On the other hand, if you delay retiring for one year until you are 66, your payments will be about 8% higher. In fact, for every year you delay receiving your Social Security, your monthly payments go up.

When will I begin to collect Social Security?

It depends on your birthday and birth year. Take a look at the chart below to see when you can start receiving full payments.

If your birthday is:	You can begin collecting at:
1/2/38- 1/1/39	65 years, 2 months
1/2/39- 1/1/40	65 years, 4 months
1/2/40- 1/1/41	65 years, 6 months
1/2/41- 1/1/42	65 years, 8 months
1/2/42- 1/1/43	65 years, 10 months
1/2/43- 1/1/55	66 years
1/2/55- 1/1/56	66 years, 2 months
1/2/56- 1/1/57	66 years, 4 months
1/2/57- 1/1/58	66 years, 6 months
1/2/58- 1/1/59	66 years, 8 months
1/2/59- 1/1/60	66 years, 10 months
1/2/60 and later	67 years

health costs

Retirees' medical bills will increase with age

Something to think about: your health care costs after you retire. **Medicare,** the federal health care program for the elderly, was established in 1965 to pay for retired people's main medical needs. But it doesn't do the whole job.

You're eligible for Medicare if you are 65 and you and/or your spouse have paid Medicare taxes at work for at least 10 years. You pay no premiums for Part A, which is hospital coverage, but you are responsible for a deductible and a (usually small) percentage of the cost of your stay. Medicare Part B is medical insurance and requires that you pay a low monthly premium ($54 in 2002). After you've satisfied the deductible ($100 in 2002), the plan pays for 80% of "reasonable and customary" charges for doctor's fees and other medical costs not covered by Part A. Some expenses are covered at 100%.

There are limitations and exclusions to Medicare coverage. Prescription drugs, eyeglasses and hearing aids, and medical care received overseas, for instance, are not generally covered. For more details on plan specifics, or for any other information about Medicare, you can call 1-800-633-4227, or visit **www.medicare.gov**.

How can you get additional medical coverage? Before you retire, check to find out if your employer offers retiree's health insurance, and what the fees are. If your company doesn't, consider, buying a **Medigap** policy, the nickname for Medicare supplemental insurance. These policies are purchased from private insurers. Congress has a number of different plans, identified by letters A to J. (Not all plans are available in every state.) The benefits provided are standardized according to the letter designation, but the cost of premiums is not, so shop around for the features you need at the right price. If you can't afford to buy supplemental insurance, check to see if you qualify for Medicaid, a state-run medical insurance plan for those with low income. It may pay some of the bills not covered by Medicare.

NURSING HOMES

At present, no federal program pays for nursing home care or home health care—what the insurance industry calls **long-term care**. Nor does Medicare or private health insurance cover the cost of long-term care. This is looming as a major problem since it is estimated that one out of three people older than 65 will need long-term care. A year in a nursing home costs anywhere from $32,000 to over $100,000. Many people use their savings to pay for nursing home care, and when their money runs out, they apply to Medicaid to pay the rest. Unfortunately, the most desirable nursing homes often resist taking Medicaid patients since Medicaid usually doesn't pay the full amount.

Whether you wind up on Medicaid or rely on it from the start, the drawback is the same: you must generally exhaust all your assets and money except your house and its furnishings, car, burial plot, and money for burial expenses before Medicaid will help you. If you plan to transfer your assets to avoid this painful situation, make sure to get professional advice.

To spare yourself having to liquidate all your savings and leave your loved ones in the financial lurch, you can buy **long-term care insurance**. It pays a daily benefit of anywhere from $50 to $250 for nursing care; less for home health care. It costs less than $1,000 per year if you first buy the policy as a 45-year-old—and climbs sharply as you age, to about $7,000 if you buy it when you are 75, depending on the type of coverage you buy. If you compare the total cost of the insurance to the cost of one year in a nursing home, the insurance is the lesser of the two.

APPLYING FOR MEDICARE

You'll automatically get your Medicare card in the mail the year you are scheduled to retire. If you want to delay retirement, notify Medicare. The number is 800-633-4227.

159

retirement homes

Should you move from your own home, or stay put?

Before you start calculating the price of a Colombian hacienda or a condo on the links, consider this: 75% of retirees stay right where they are. They're comfortable in houses and communities where they may have lived for years, and fear they'll be lonely far away from their friends, children, or grandchildren.

If you do prefer to retire to some bucolic spot, you'll want to check the tax rates and the cost of living in the communities you consider. Picking a cheaper region might yield a special windfall: when you trade down to a cheaper house, your profit is tax free (up to $250,000 for a single person and $500,000 for a married couple), as long as you've been living in the house you're selling for two of the last five years.

A few retirees—about 6%—choose formal retirement communities. These are age-restricted, sometimes gated housing developments that may have the feel of country clubs, with social directors, lavish pools, and field trips; or they may be city high rises. In some, you rent your house or apartment; in others, you buy the property for anywhere from $40,000 up. The best ones have 24-hour skilled

nursing care in nearby buildings. Some, called continuing care communities, also have assisted-living and/or nursing home facilities where you're guaranteed a place if your health begins to deteriorate in later years.

ASK THE EXPERTS

How can I afford to stay in my home after I retire?

Decide how you'll pay for property and income taxes. High-tax states like Massachusetts and New York nibble away at your savings faster than do low-or no-tax ones like New Hampshire and Texas. You also might consider turning part of your home into a rental unit or taking in a roommate.

Would a reverse mortgage be a good idea?

Sometimes. A reverse mortgage—also known as a home equity conversion—is a mortgage in which a bank loans you a lump sum or monthly payments while you live in your house. Either way, you still own the house and may live in it. When you die, the bank loan becomes due and the home is generally sold to settle the debt. If your heirs want the house, they have to pay the bank.

What if I want to live abroad?

You'll probably get more for your money. Country farmhouses in Umbria, Italy, sell for as little as $32,000, as do Spanish colonial cottages in the artsy Mexican town of San Miguel de Allende. But you're on your own in paying for health care; Medicare won't cover you in another country. And you may want a health insurance policy that includes emergency evacuation to the United States.

How can I plan for a time when I'm too old to live on my own?

It's tough to admit that one day you'll shelve your skis and tennis racquet, and maybe even stop driving your car. That you may need a place that offers meals, as well as medical help should you need it. These retirement places are called assisted living facilities. They offer a middle level of care, between retirement communities and nursing homes. A drawback: many assisted living residences require a large up-front deposit.

now what do I do?

Answers to common questions

One retirement calculator says I should save $2,500 per year to reach my goal; another says $5,000. How can I tell which one is right?

Calculators—designed by human financial planners and analysts—all work on a "what if" basis. Planners who figure you'll get no Social Security, earn a modest 8% percent return on your investments, and live to age 90 will tell you to save more than those who think you'll get Social Security, earn a happy 10% return and live to age 84. In general, gravitate toward the most conservative estimates. It's obviously more pleasant to wind up having too much.

Where can I buy long-term care insurance?

Most private insurance companies offer it. Look for a company that has been providing it for 10 years, and has a good record in paying claims. Also check to make sure your policy offers the most flexible qualifications for coverage. For example, your plan should cover care (personal as well as medical) at home or in a nursing home, and should not exclude pre-existing conditions. The premiums on policies may be tax deductible. Contact the National Council on Aging at 202-479-1200 for more information on long-term care insurance.

How can I tell the difference between a good nursing home and one that will mistreat me or rip me off?

The American Association of Homes and Services for the Aging, a trade group of nursing home operators, accredits 230 nursing homes. Get the list from the Continuing Care Accreditation Commission, 901 E Street, NW, Suite 500, Washington, DC 20004. Contact them before you sign up with a nursing home.

I'm nervous about all the taxes when I retire. Should I hire an accountant?

With all these tax rules and regulations, it's easy to see how valuable a session with a tax accountant (see page 142) or financial planner (see page 74) can be. It's worth paying a few dollars to map out the most advantageous way to tap into the various retirement funds you have, while paying the minimum in taxes.

I'd like some professional retirement planning advice.

Fee-only financial planners—those you pay by the hour—are in a position to be more unbiased in their recommendations than planners who charge little or nothing, but who earn most of their living from the commissions that mutual funds, banks, and insurance companies pay them to sell their products. The following associations can refer you to planners in your area:

Fee and non-fee planners:

Financial Planning Association
5775 Glenridge Drive, NE Suite B300
Atlanta, GA 30328
Tel: 800-322-4237 (**www.fpanet.org**)

Fee-only planners:

National Association of Personal Financial Advisors
355 Dundee Road, Suite 200
Buffalo Grove, IL 60089
Tel: 800-366-2732 (**www.napfa.org**)

Certified Professional Accountants (CPAs) who are also financial planners:

The American Institute of CPAs
1211 Avenue of the Americas
New York, NY 10036
Tel: 800-862-4272 (**www.aicpa.org**)

HELPFUL RESOURCES

BOOKS

You've Earned it, Don't Lose It
by Suze Orman

The Retirement Source Book
by Mary Helen and Shuford Smith

50 Fabulous Places to Retire in America
by Lee and Laralee Rosenberg

Choose a College Town for Retirement
by Joseph Lubow

Family finance

FAMILY FINANCES

9

" Seventy percent of Americans have no written will or estate plan. Don't be one of them. "

kids and money

Covering all the changes

Great, you've started to get your financial house in order. And then along comes baby and, wow, who knew how expensive it would be. Here are some money-saving tips:

1. Clothes. Try to stay away from paying full retail prices on clothes that your child will only outgrow in a few months. Shop at discount clothing stores or secondhand clothing shops. Don't be shy about hand-me-downs from family and friends—most will be glad to get rid of the clothes and pleased they're going to a child they know.

2. Equipment. Babies need transportation items: car seat, stroller. Then there's the highchair and crib. Again these items are going to be needed only for a few years. Shop at discount baby stores or try thrift stores. Same goes for equipment older kids need, such as bikes and swing sets.

3. Toys. Well-meaning friends and family often bombard little ones with flashy new games and trinkets. Let them. The trick is to show your child that there is fun to be had with everyday things, too. When the little ones turn two or three, take a box of ziti pasta and have them separate them into different colored plastic containers. Later, you can paint the ziti and string the pieces together to make a necklace. Or go outside and paint rocks to create a rock garden. These "found" toys are easy and fun to play with.

KIDS AND TAXES

Don't worry, this won't be too painful. It's just important to know some of the tax consequences and benefits your darling is creating. If this is too overwhelming, hire a tax pro to help you sort it out (see page 142). For the brave of heart, here's an overview of what you need to know:

Personal exemption: As soon as your baby arrives, you get to take him or her as a personal exemption of $3,000, which ends up saving you $300 to $1,100 depending on your tax bracket.

Kiddie tax: No doubt you've already thought, well, since my little one is only five, he has to be in a lower tax bracket than I am. Why not put my investments in his name and pay tax at his tax rate instead of mine? Good idea, but the IRS is wise to it and issued a cut-off of $1,500. In other words, any investment income Junior makes above that amount gets taxed at your tax rate, not his. Sorry.

Custodian account: If you decide you want to put money in your child's name, then you need to set up a custodian account, known as UTMA (Uniform Transfers to Minors Act) or UGMA (Uniform Gifts to Minors Act). You can set it up via your bank, your brokerage house, or your mutual fund provider.

Child and dependent care credits: If mom goes back to work and pays a day care center or qualified childcare provider, she can recoup 20% to 30% of those costs from her taxes. See page 139. (Some corporations also offer pre-tax dependent care expense accounts for childcare. If you take advantage of that you can't claim it on your taxes.)

kids and spending

Teach them how to save, as well as spend

Sometimes it can feel like there's a war going on for your paycheck. Your 17-year-old is nagging you for a car, but you think every dime should go toward saving for college. Your 9-year-old daughter wants horseback-riding and ice-skating lessons, and your spouse thinks this is the year for the Grand Canyon.

One great way to minimize the stress is to set family priorities. Try this exercise: draw three columns on a piece of paper, and label them "essential," "very important," and "wish list." With your spouse, figure the cost of the essentials, such as rent or mortgage payments, utilities, transportation expenses, debt, and basic grocery bills. Next discuss what goes on your "very important" list. What are your key financial goals? College? Retirement in a certain number of years? Helping an aging parent? Redecorating the living room?

Relegate all other items to the wish list. There's probably more here than you can afford, of course. And you and your spouse might disagree about some items. But at least you have a draft. Now call a family meeting. One way to cap children's requests is to get them to make choices: what three things would they like to do, have, or buy most this month or year? Put that in the wish list column. This way, children don't feel deprived—they get their wishes heard.

Now comes the hard part: Ask older children what they'd give up in order to have a dream item. Is your son willing to work full time for a year during college in order to have the Mustang now? Is your teenage daughter willing to cook dinner every Wednesday night, so she can have the prom dress of her dreams? Some items could be family wishes, like an outing or swing set that everyone agrees to save for. When negotiations are complete, have everyone sign a copy of the family plan. Ideally, this plan can help everyone think of money and spending as a family project.

ALL ABOUT ALLOWANCES

Experts almost universally favor giving children an allowance starting at about age five, so they can learn about money's value. How much should you give a child for his or her allowance? On that, nobody agrees. One rule of thumb is to give a dollar a week for each school grade—$1 for first graders, $4 for fourth graders, and so forth. Other experts think it should be much less. Of course, the amount also depends on what you can afford.

The point of an allowance is to teach the value of money. Children should be able to spend it as they choose, and not be told to use it for lunch or for a necessary item of clothing, such as socks or sandals.

To cope with those overpriced items teens crave, like trendy sneakers and designer-label jeans, try a quarterly clothing allowance. You put no restrictions on what they buy, but make it clear that the money—say, $200—has to cover all their clothes for that quarter. Parents report that when teens are forced to wear the same two shirts over and over because they couldn't pass up the $80 pair of pants or $50 pair of earrings, they think more carefully about future luxury purchases.

60 SECONDS $ SAVINGS

Older children can learn about money by playing financially-oriented board games such as Monopoly. Once you know a bit about investing yourself, you might set up a small stock account for an older child, and let him invest in companies that make products he likes—favorite clothes, books, movies, and toys.

estate planning

A little planning can make a lot of difference

How do you protect your family financially if something happens to you? One way is to do a little planning so that the money you have passes to your family as smoothly as possible. Lawyers and accountants have a fancy name for this. They call it estate planning. That might sound grand—as though you had a country home and a stable full of horses—but it only means making sure your money and assets, however modest, are inherited by the people you have chosen to have them. And more importantly, they will not have to pay estate tax on what you give them.

The good news is that the government is scaling back how much estate tax it charges. For starters, if your estate is worth $1,000,000 or less, your heirs pay no tax on it in 2002. By the year 2009, it's $3.5 million that's tax free. Congress lets you leave an unlimited fortune to your spouse or to charity, but if you wish to leave any of your assets to your children, they must pay estate tax on any amount over the limit. What exactly do your heirs pay estate tax on? Your net worth, which is the amount of your assets minus your liabilities, plus life insurance. To figure out your net worth, add up your assets and subtract any debt or taxes you owe. See the next page for help.

FIRST PERSON   DISASTER STORY

No Will, No Way

When I was growing up, my Aunt Sadie lived with our family. She was what they used to call a "maiden lady" and I loved her dearly. I had always loved a beautiful emerald ring that her mother had given her many years before. Aunt Sadie wore that ring every day, and she told me time and again that some day that lovely ring would be mine. Unfortunately, my aunt died without leaving a will. There was no written record that the ring was meant for me, and her two other nieces, my cousins, had no intention of letting me have it—especially since there were no other significant assets. The court split her estate among the nieces, and the ring had to be sold so we'd all get some money. It bothers me a lot that a stranger is wearing my aunt's ring today—all because she neglected to leave a will. That's a mistake I know I won't make.

Cindy F., Bay Shore, New York

STEP BY STEP: FIGURING YOUR NET WORTH

1. Add up all your assets, or what you own:
- Money in the bank
- Investments (stocks, bonds, mutual funds)
- IRAs
- Your company pension plan money owed to beneficiaries upon your death
- 401(k) funds
- The value of your house (based on current market price) ✓
- Cars
- Jewelry ✓
- Furniture, heirlooms, art

2. Add up your liabilities, or what you owe:
- Mortgage
- Credit card debt
- Taxes
- Loans

3. To get your total net worth:
Subtract your liabilities from your assets. If this amount, plus any life insurance proceeds, is over $1,000,000 in the year 2002 and you leave it to anyone other than a spouse or charity, estate taxes will be owed.

your will

Think of it as a list of your wishes

A will is a legal document that specifies who will get your money and property after you die. Why have one? Because if you die without a will, the government takes control of your estate and a court decides who gets your stuff. The case could get tied up in a long, painful, and costly court proceeding; by the time your heirs see any money, a big chunk of it is likely to have gone to the court-appointed lawyers.

Seventy percent of Americans have no written will or estate plan. Don't be one of them. The simplest kind of will—often called an "I love you" will—is one in which you leave everything to your spouse. But if you're widowed, divorced, or single, you need to be more specific about who inherits what.

When you draw up a will, you must name an executor—the person who sees to it that your wishes are carried out. Typically, people name a spouse, an adult child, or a trusted relative or friend. If no one close to you seems appropriate, or if you think your will might be disputed, you might name a lawyer or banker.

You also should think about whether you want to have a living will. This is a legal document that instructs doctors not to prolong your life artificially, and describes the degree to which you want medical caregivers to use life support measures. Simultaneously, give someone health care power of attorney. This is a person empowered to make decisions about your medical care—and your life—if you become incapacitated.

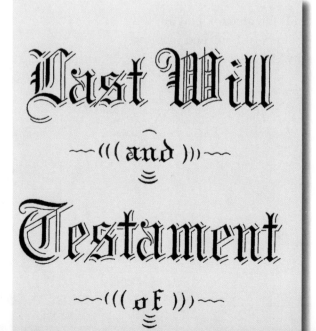

Last Will
~ (((and))) ~

Testament
~ (((of))) ~

ASK THE EXPERTS

Can I write my own will?

You could, but probably shouldn't. If you decide to experiment with kits and books, at least have a lawyer review your work. Otherwise, you risk creating an invalid will and your wishes might not prevail. Handwritten wills are not valid in quite a few states.

What if I need to make changes to my will a few years after I have drawn it up?

Changes to a will are called codicils. They are necessary if there is a major change in your family; for example, the birth of another child or the sale of an important asset listed in the will, such as a business. The addition of codicils needs to have your signature as well as the signatures of two witnesses.

What if I have no living relatives?

You can leave your estate to charities, schools you attended, friends, even pets. Otherwise, your assets will go to the state.

How can I find the right lawyer?

Look for one who specializes in trusts and estate planning. Asking for referrals from trusted friends and associates is one smart way to go. Call the American Academy of Estate Planning at 800-846-1555. Or contact their Web site at **www.aaepa.com**.

Should I set up a trust for my children?

Maybe, especially if your children are young and you have significant assets. This way you can help provide for their college educations. A trust is especially appropriate if you have a disabled child who may never be able to earn his own living.

what's probate?

How your assets get to the right heir

How do your assets get distributed to your heirs and your debts paid off? Through probate court. The job of the probate court is to make sure your will is valid (signed and witnessed correctly), that all taxes and outstanding debts have been paid, all taxes filed for the current year, and all your wishes carried out. (You can avoid probate only if you leave all your assets to your spouse.)

During probate, the court will appoint a personal representative or executor, usually the person you've named in your will. It's the executor's job to see the case through court, usually with the help of an attorney, and to carry out the wishes stated in your will.

Some key responsibilities of the executor are to:

■ Open and inventory the deceased person's safe deposit box according to the laws of the state

■ Get copies of the death certificate

■ Inventory all assets, policies, and funds

■ Process payments of taxes, and any valid claims of creditors

■ Keep records of funeral expenses

■ Notify the Social Security Administration of the death, and find out whether any survivor benefits are available

■ Employ any necessary professionals needed to assist, such as lawyers and accountants

■ Get the names, addresses, and Social Security numbers of all persons named in the will, and distribute the inheritance

■ Make funeral arrangements, if the family hasn't done it

■ Put a death notice in the local paper

BEATING THE FUNERAL INDUSTRY

The average price of a funeral is $4,800, according to industry figures, but costs often can be double that. Meanwhile, consumer advocates say you can cut the bill to as little as $1,500 with some advance planning, comparison shopping, and negotiations.

The golden rule is to plan your own funeral and burial in advance. To do that, speak with several different funeral homes, and then lock in a deal and provide for it financially in your estate. This will save your loved ones from falling victim to funeral directors who mark up expenses tenfold, tack on mysterious fees, and present your family with a $15,000 bill. If calling around is too overwhelming, then at least specify what type of burial you would like, either interment or cremation. ash

Very important: once you've made your plans, write them down and leave them in an accessible place, perhaps an office drawer that holds important papers. Tell your loved ones where these papers are. Do not store them where you keep your will. Wills are not usually looked at until after the funeral.

The golden rule is to plan your own funeral and burial in advance.

now what do I do?

Answers to common questions

How much do funerals cost? Should I say in my will that my estate will pay for it?

Prices vary widely— from $1,500 or so if you shop around in advance and insist on a modest service, to upwards of $10,000 if you run into avaricious funeral directors, want a fancy farewell scene, or just leave the project to your heirs. Yes, ideally, your estate should pay for it—that way you don't put the burden on your heirs.

My elderly mother is giving away all her money. Can I get power of attorney to manage her affairs?

That's tricky. If she's in good health, mentally sound, and doesn't want your advice, you can't just take over: how she spends her money is up to her. If, however, she's losing her mental faculties, you either could persuade her to sign a legal form giving you power of attorney, under which you or another person would become responsible for the financial management of her estate, or petition in court to show she is mentally incapable. If the court agrees that she is, it will appoint a guardian to manage her affairs, usually in this order of priority: 1) spouse 2) adult children 3) parents 4) adult siblings.

How long does probate take?

Anywhere from a few weeks to two years, depending on the complexity of the estate and the efficiency of the court.

How can I avoid probate?

One of the things probate does is transfer title of goods from you to your heirs. To avoid that procedure, set up your accounts so that transfer happens immediately upon your death. Change the title from just your name to either joint tenancy or tenancy by the entirety. You also can set up pay-on-death accounts. To do that, make sure all your bank accounts, government securities, and investment securities have a designated beneficiary of your choosing. The money remains in your complete control until your death. Another way to avoid probate is to set up a living trust.

What are some common ways to minimize estate taxes?

An estate planning attorney probably would suggest things like creating a Credit Shelter Trust, a Charitable Trust, or giving away assets during your lifetime.

Can a living trust save me money on estate taxes?

Not necessarily. In order to save estate taxes, you need to create certain provisions called Credit Shelters that take effect at your death. These provisions can be included in either your will or a living trust.

Where should I keep my living will?

Living wills are essentially your instructions to medical professionals not to prolong your life artificially. For this reason, leave a copy of it with your primary care physician and your local hospital. It's also a good idea to have a note in your wallet stating that you have a living will and where it is located.

HELPFUL RESOURCES

WEB SITES	BOOKS
www.nolo.com Site offers info on wills and estate planning.	**How Can I Ever Afford to Have Children?** by Barbara Hetzer
www.funerals.org Site of the Funeral Consumers Alliance; it can help you find a funeral home.	**Kids, Parents and Money: Teaching Personal Finance from Piggy Bank to Prom** by Willard and William Stawski
www.netplanning.com/consumer/ Information about estate planning.	**Financial Fitness for Life** by Jerry Mason
	The Complete Book of Wills, Estates, and Trusts by Alexander A. Bove

get it together

Putting your
financial
house in Order

1 Pay off your credit card debt. This is the single biggest obstacle to financial progress. As soon as you can remove this black hole from your pocketbook, you'll find the other steps a cakewalk.

2 Start tracking where your money goes. Another key starting point: keep a spending journal. You'll never be able to change your spending and saving habits until you know what your current ones are!

3 Figure out your financial goals. Before you read a map, you need to know where you're starting from (that's why you need a record of your expenses). But you also need to know where you're going. These are your financial goals.

4 Create a budget. Once you have a handle on your income and spending habits, make a plan for spending and saving to help you meet the goals you identified. This is your budget.

5 Pay yourself first. Since you'll never feel like you have enough money to start saving, you might as well start now. If you want to build your emergency fund, or if you have short-term goals like owning a car or taking a vacation or if you plan to buy a house soon, make sure your budget includes these—and then take action and start saving!

6 **Put away money for retirement.** Your budget probably includes some allowance for retirement savings (if it doesn't, it should). Now it's time to implement: Sign up for your company's 401(k) plan. You can contribute as little as 1% of your salary—a painless way to start. If your company doesn't have one, open an IRA and start stashing. Saving as little as $50 a month will get you going.

7 **Take care of your insurance needs.** If you're just starting out, disability insurance should be your top priority. Once you have kids, though, make sure you review your life insurance needs, and possibly long-term care insurance.

8 **Get your taxes in order.** If you panic at tax time, get your records together early and hire a tax adviser to help you sort through them. If you pay a lot in taxes, look for smart ways to save. But don't start incurring expenses just to save on taxes. Remember: if your tax bill is high, it means you're making a lot of money. That's a good thing!

9 **Draw up a will, living will, and health care power of attorney.** Just as taxes are inevitable, so is death. By planning ahead for this inevitability, your spouse and other heirs will have one less thing to worry about if something happens to you.

10 **Take your investments to the next level.** This is where most people want to start, since it's the most exciting—especially when the market is hot. The smart thing to do, however, is to start by putting your money only in investments you are comfortable with and understand. Once all the other pieces are in place, then revisit your investments and dig deeper into the nuts and bolts of stocks, bonds, mutual funds, and other investments.

Note: These ten things to do are not in descending order of importance. Start with what you need to do first.

glossary

Adjusted Gross Income (AGI) This is a tax term for all of your income (salary, interest, dividends, retirement income, etc.), adjusted for certain items, like contributions to IRAs and self-employed retirement plans, alimony payments, deductible student loan interest, and deductible moving expenses. The significance? It's used in many calculations to figure out if you can take certain deductions and credits.

After-tax Income Your take-home salary is an example of after-tax income—money that has already been subject to income taxes. That means if you take your paycheck to the bank or invest it in the stock market, you only have to pay tax on the amount you earn, over and above the original investment. On the other hand, when you put money in a 401(k) or deductible IRA, you're using pre-tax income, since that money hasn't been taxed yet. That means when you pull it out, you have to pay tax on all of it.

AGI See Adjusted Gross Income.

Annual Report Once a year all publicly traded companies have to give their owners (shareholders) a state-of-the-company address known as the annual report. It includes financial and other information about the past year's performance as well as the CEO's analysis of the company's past and future outlook.

Annuity This is an investment that guarantees income payments to its owner, for the owner's life. When an investor buys an annuity (using after-tax dollars), his investment grows tax-deferred until he begins to withdraw money from the account. Of course, there's a cost to the guaranteed income and the tax-deferred growth: commissions, administrative fees, surrender charges, and early withdrawal penalties often make annuities a wise investment for only a small number of people.

Asset This is essentially anything of value. Examples include your bank accounts, investments, house, and jewelry.

Bankruptcy If someone is completely unable to pay his debts, he has the option of declaring bankruptcy. Sometimes this means creating a formal (court-assisted) plan for repaying debts, known as Chapter 13. The other option is Chapter 7, which wipes out most debts. Under this type, the person's credit rating is more severely damaged, and the person isn't allowed to keep as much of his assets.

Beneficiary A beneficiary is the person who benefits from being named on a life insurance policy or an IRA, 401(k), or SEP IRA, account. If the owner of the policy or account dies, the money is transferred to the person named.

Blue Chip These are stocks of large U.S. companies with long-term track records that have a reputation for stable, steady growth, dividend payments, and tried and true products and services.

Bond Essentially a loan from a government or company to an individual, a bond is a promise to pay a fixed amount of interest for the use of someone else's money, for a fixed period of time. For this reason, bonds are known as "fixed income" investments. The "face value" or "principal" is the amount the investor loans to the bond issuer; the "coupon" is the amount of interest the issuer pays to the bondholder. The date the loan must be repaid is arranged in advance and is known as the bond's "maturity date."

Broker Whether you make your own decisions or listen to an advisor, you need a broker to buy stocks and bonds. If you come up with your own ideas, discount brokers can execute the trades for you. If you want someone to do the research for you, you need a full-service broker. Their commissions generally are higher than those of discount brokers.

Capital Gains Tax When your stocks increase in value, the profit you make is a form of income called a capital gain. If you sell the stock, you owe tax—the capital gains tax—on the difference between the price you paid for it and the price you sold it for. This tax generally applies to any investment you sell for more than you paid. If you hold your investment for more than one year, the capital gain is considered long term, and is taxed at better rates than your other income. If you hold it less than one year, it's considered short term, and is taxed just like your other income.

Capitalization See Market Capitalization.

Collateral This is any asset you pledge to the bank (or other money lender) in return for a loan. If you default (don't repay the loan), the collateral is given to the bank to help satisfy your debt.

Commodity These are bulk goods traded on exchanges. Typical examples include metals (like gold and silver), grains (like corn and wheat), and meats (like beef and pork).

Coupon See Bond.

Credit Report A credit report is a detailed tracking of your debt repayment history. It includes information about how you've paid utility companies, credit cards, and other businesses. This report is used when other companies are deciding whether or not to extend credit to you.

Debit Card It acts like a credit card; but rather than running up a tab for you to pay at the end of each month, a debit card pulls money right out of your checking account each time you buy something with it.

Defined Benefit Pension Plan A retirement plan that pays long-time employees a specific amount of money (a defined benefit) each month, when they retire. It's highly desirable, since employees don't have to contribute any money to this plan in order to benefit from it.

Defined Contribution Pension Plan This is a name for a 401(k) or similar plan. These plans generally rely on you (the employee) to make regular (defined) contributions to your own account, which grows tax-deferred until you need the money, usually after retirement. The amount you receive at retirement depends on how well the account's investments performed.

Dependents People who depend on you, usually your children or elderly parents, for financial support. In order to qualify as a dependent, the person must meet certain requirements (income, citi-

zenship, relationship and others). Claiming dependents can be a tax saver (as long as your AGI is less than $259,800 if you're single, $328,500 if you're married).

Dividend An added bonus to some stock investments, dividends are a part of a company's profits returned to the shareholders. Mutual funds also pay dividends to their shareholders, based on the income of the fund's underlying stocks and bonds.

Dividend Yield See Yield.

Equity 1. This is another term for stocks. 2. If you're talking about home equity, this is the difference between what you could sell your home for and the current amount of your mortgage.

Estate Planning Not something only for the super-rich, estate planning is the process of planning for the disposition and administration of assets at a person's death (or if mentally or physically incompetent), something that applies to many people.

Estate Tax If you die with "too much" money and don't qualify for certain deductions, the IRS will levy estate taxes on the assets you leave behind. You're allowed to leave as much as you want to your spouse or to charity, and the first $1,000,000 beyond that is also exempt. But after that, this hefty tax—37% to 55%—kicks in.

Executor This is the person named in a will to handle all of a deceased person's financial affairs, or estate.

Face Value See Bond.

Federal Reserve System Also called "the Fed," the system consists of 12 Federal Reserve Banks and a board that governs its decisions. The Fed oversees the entire United States money and banking system. It regulates the money supply, imposes certain rules on banks, and runs the federal Mint that prints money. When it raises or lowers the interest rates for its 12 banks, there is a ripple effect throughout the economy.

Fixed Income See Bond.

Fund Manager A mutual fund's main decision maker, the manager's ability to pick stocks and read the economy is often a key factor in a fund's success.

General Obligation Bond This is the safest type of municipal bond issued by state and local governments. Its safety comes from the government's ability to tax residents and, therefore, it is unlikely to default on these bonds. Also see Revenue Bonds.

Index These are groups of traded stocks that help investors figure out how their stocks are performing, relative to other, similar stocks. Common indices include Standard & Poor's 500 stocks (S&P 500), the Dow Jones Industrial Average (DJIA), and the National Association of Securities Dealers Automated Quotations (NASDAQ composite).

Individual Retirement Account See IRA.

Inflation A measurement of how fast the prices of goods and services are rising.

Inside Information Important facts about or decisions made within a company that have not been made public but that may affect the company's value, such as a merger with another company. A company's employees (and their relatives) are not allowed to pass this information to others or use it themselves to make stock trades.

Interest The amount a lender charges a borrower for the use of his money. Simple interest is based on the principal only. Compound interest, on the other hand, is based on the amount of principal, plus any accumulated interest.

IPO Initial Public Offering. This is the process where smaller businesses that are privately owned by one or more people raise a lot of money by selling stock to the public. This is usually done on major exchanges, like the New York Stock Exchange (NYSE), American Stock Exchange (ASE), or NASDAQ. Although they own a smaller percentage of the company after the IPO, the company has a lot more cash to use to grow the business. It also creates a liquid market for their stock, if they want to sell it later.

IRA Investors use Individual Retirement Accounts to stash money for retirement. Interest and dividends that are earned in this type of account aren't taxed until the owner withdraws the money, usually after retirement. Types of IRAs include traditional, Roth, and Education.

IRS The Internal Revenue Service is the governmental body that's in charge of collecting taxes on behalf of the federal government.

Issuer This is the corporation or government entity that generates money to spend by selling bonds to investors, and promising to make timely interest payments and principal repayments.

Itemized Deductions Mortgage interest, real estate taxes, charitable contributions, add up to significant tax reductions. Even though it can mean a more complicated tax return, it's often more beneficial than taking the standard deduction.

Kiddie Tax This is imposed on kids under 14 who have dividends, interest, or other investment income. If they have more than $1,500 of this type of income, it's taxed at their parent's rate (usually 27% to 39%), rather than their own low rate (10%).

Large Cap Short for large capitalization stocks, these stocks tend to be more stable than smaller company stocks, and typically are traded on the New York Stock Exchange or the American Stock Exchange. They often pay dividends, and generally have market capitalizations of $5 billion or more.

Life Insurance In exchange for annual payments (or "premiums"), a life insurance company issues a contract (or "policy") that promises to pay a fixed amount when the policy's owner dies. The payment is made to the person listed in the policy as the beneficiary. Term policy premiums stay low for a fixed number of years (usually five to 30), then usually rise dramatically if the owner wants to keep the policy in place. Permanent policy premiums start out higher than term premiums, but stay level for the owner's entire life. Permanent policies also have a savings component, called the cash value, that builds over time.

Liquidity If it's easy to find buyers or sellers of a particular stock or bond, it's considered liquid. This makes an investment more attractive.

Long-term Capital Gains See Capital Gains Tax.

Margin Account This is a brokerage account that allows its owner to borrow money in order to buy more stocks and bonds. While it can boost profits, buying on margin is also very risky.

Market Capitalization The value of a company, which is determined by multiplying the stock's current price by the number of outstanding shares.

Maturity Date See Bond.

Mid Cap Short for middle-level capitalization, mid-cap stocks generally have capitalizations of between $1 billion and $5 billion.

Municipal Bond Issued by state and local governments, municipal (or "muni") bonds generally are not taxed by the federal government. Since this makes them more attractive, munis can get away with paying investors less than other bonds.

Mutual Fund When an investment company pulls together many investors to pool their money to buy stocks and bonds, a mutual fund is born, and its investors (or shareholders) are able to diversify better than if they were on their own.

NASDAQ National Association of Securities Dealers Automated Quotation is a computerized stock market listing. Generally these stocks are for companies that aren't big enough to trade on the New York, American, or other listed stock exchanges. Trading procedures for NASDAQ stocks are a little different from those for the listed exchange-traded stocks.

Net Asset Value How do mutual funds determine their prices? A fund's net asset value, or NAV, is like its price. It's determined by taking the value of all of the fund's underlying stocks, bonds, etc., and dividing it by the total number of shares owned by investors.

No-load Mutual Fund Commissions that brokers charge investors to buy a mutual fund are called "loads." So, no-load funds don't make you pay a commission in order to invest. Generally these funds are bought directly from the mutual fund company rather than through a middleman.

Option These somewhat risky investments allow investors the choice—or the option—of buying a stock at a predetermined price at a later date. Buying a stock option costs money, but if the price of the stock rises above the "strike price" (the purchase price you've locked in), you can make money by "exercising" the option (buying the stock at the lower preset price) and then selling it for a profit. On the other hand, if you buy an option for a stock whose price goes down, the option will "expire," worthless.

Overdraft When you write a check or try to withdraw funds beyond the amount of money you have in your account. This usually results in hefty charges or fees.

Pension Plans See Defined Benefit Plan and Defined Contribution Plan.

PMI Mortgage lenders usually require Private Mortgage Insurance (PMI) when you buy a home without putting down at least 20% of the purchase price for the down payment. This insurance will pay the lender if you can't meet your mortgage payments.

Portfolio Manager A generic term for someone who makes investment decisions for a large pool of money. Examples of companies that hire portfolio managers include mutual funds, insurance companies, pension plans, and banks' trust departments.

Power of Attorney A written, legally binding document that gives another person the right to make financial or health decisions on your behalf.

Premium If you buy a bond for more than its face value, you're paying a premium for the difference between your cost and the face value.

Pre-tax Income See After-tax Income.

Prime Rate This is the interest rate that banks charge their best customers, usually businesses, for loans. Often loans to other customers are tied to this rate; for example, "Prime plus one" means a loan whose interest rate is one percentage point higher than the bank's prime lending rate.

Principal See Bond.

Probate This is the long and winding road heirs must follow through the court system to carry out the deceased's wishes, as made known in her will.

Prospectus Used most frequently by mutual funds, this little booklet (required to be given to potential investors) includes information about the fund's management, objectives, and past performance.

Publicly Traded A stock that's publicly traded has some or all of its shares held by public investors, as opposed to private investors, and can be bought and sold on the exchange on which it's listed. These companies have to follow many reporting requirements and other regulations.

Recession A downturn in the economy.

Replacement Cost If you need to make an insurance claim, replacement cost insurance pays you the amount of money it takes to replace the item(s) that were lost, stolen, or damaged. If you don't have replacement cost coverage, the company might pay only the amount that the item was currently worth, which might not be enough to actually replace it.

Revenue Bond This type of municipal bond is not backed by the issuing government's ability to tax—it's backed by a particular project that's supposed to generate revenue. This means that if the project doesn't produce the income expected, the bondholders might not receive the expected income payments—or worse: they might not get their principal back. See also General Obligation Bond.

Rider An attachment to an insurance policy that changes its terms or conditions is a "rider."

Risk Your investment might not increase as you expect it to; or worse, it could end up losing money. This possibility is known as risk. Investors accept risk, however, because they believe that the possible payoff (or "return") ultimately will be worthwhile.

Return on investment Also known as ROI. When you invest money in stocks, bonds, and mutual funds, you eventually want to get back more than you invested. The amount you get back, over and above your beginning investment, is called your return. If you divide your return by the amount you originally invested, you can calculate the percentage of your "return on investment." Knowing this percentage helps you compare investments.

Roth IRA Named after the senator who invented it, the Roth IRA is an individual retirement account that doesn't allow an up-front deduction (like a traditional IRA). Instead, this nifty IRA uses after-tax dollars to fund it, so when the money is withdrawn during retirement, the investor doesn't have to pay tax on the money it earned over the years.

Savings Bond Issued by the U.S. government, savings bonds are sold at most banks and cost half of their face value. They don't make interest payments, per se, but they do increase in value each year. When you receive the face value at maturity, the difference between what you originally paid for it, and the amount you get back, is considered interest income and is taxed on your federal income tax (but not your state income tax).

SEC The Securities and Exchange Commission is a federal agency that enforces the rules and regulations for selling investments. Its goal is to make sure investors are given the basic information needed to make good investment decisions, and to protect them against malpractice in the stock and bond markets.

SEP IRA A Simplified Employee Pension (SEP)

allows self-employed people and small business owners to set up retirement plans that work like a 401(k), but aren't subject to as many rules, regulations, and administrative details. These plans generally allow self-employed individuals to sock away up to 20% of their net business income, up to a maximum of $40,000 per year.

Shareholder This is someone who owns part of a company or mutual fund. (A "share" of stock or mutual fund is a unit of ownership that the person actually owns.)

Short-term Capital Gain See Capital Gains Tax.

SIMPLE IRA Geared toward small business owners who want to contribute to their employees' retirement accounts, Simple IRAs are similar to 401(k) plans, but they're not as popular as SEP IRAs.

Small Cap Short for small capitalization stocks, these high-risk stocks can have the potential to earn higher returns. They are frequently traded over the NASDAQ

Standard Deduction If you don't specify (or "itemize") your deductions on your income tax return, you can take the standard deduction, which is a minimum fixed amount that all taxpayers are entitled to deduct.

Stock This is a type of investment that represents ownership in a company.

Stock Split When a stock splits, it's like cutting a pie into smaller pieces: the number of shares in the company increases (often doubles), and the value per share decreases (often about in half). But because nothing about the company really changes (just like nothing about the pie changes), the value of your stock holdings generally stays the same.

Taxable Income This is the amount of your total income that you have to pay tax on, after all possible deductions have been taken.

Tax Credit Certain credits are allowed to offset your tax bill, dollar for dollar. Some of these are: a $600 credit for each child under age 17; income tax paid to a foreign government; and education credits for certain college costs for you or your children.

Tax-deferred Interest, dividends, and other gains aren't subject to taxation in these types of accounts until the owner withdraws money from them, usually after retirement.

Trust This is a very general term that describes a wide range of vehicles used to own property. Trusts generally don't save money on taxes. They're used mostly when someone wants to put restrictions or parameters on how their property is to be used, managed, and distributed to others.

Volatility The price fluctuation of a stock, bond, or other asset.

Yield Refers to the percent of income an asset is paying. A stock's yield is called the "dividend yield," and is calculated by taking the amount of dividend the company pays and dividing it by the stock's price. A bond's "yield to maturity" is a little trickier to calculate—it's usually given to you by a broker. It represents the bond's total return, if you hold it until it matures.

index

THE AUTHOR: UP CLOSE

Barbara Loos learned about money the hard way—as a reporter at *Fortune* magazine where she worked on various stories, including the "Fortune International 500." She has written for *Euromoney* and numerous other financial magazines. She would like to thank financial planner Hope Egan for her keen insight, as well as Eric Kaufman and Jack Zitomer for their help.

Barbara J. Morgan Publisher, Silver Lining Books

Barnes & Noble Basics™

Barb Chintz Editorial Director

Leonard Vigliarolo Design Director

Barnes & Noble Basics™ *Saving Money*

Nancy Condry Editor

Mary D'Ambrosio, Carol Dannhauser, Hope Egan, Cinda Siler Contributing Writers

Ann Stewart Picture Research

Emily Seese Editorial Assistant

Della R. Mancuso Production Manager